Company's Coming®

Appetizers & Snacks

Jean Paré

www.companyscoming.com
visit our website

Front Cover

1. Sweet Potato Chips
   with Scallops and
   Pea Purée,
   page 42

Back Cover

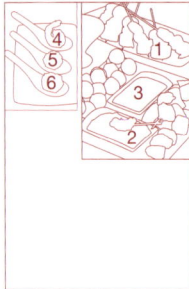

1. Mango Veggie Skewers,
   page 110
2. Falafel with Curry Yogurt,
   page 122
3. Bourbon Chicken Bites,
   page 130
4. Stuffed Shrimp,
   page 50
5. Grape Pistachio Bites,
   page 32
6. Coconut Crab Cakes,
   page 45

Appetizers & Snacks

Copyright © Company's Coming Publishing Limited

First Printing October 2012

Library and Archives Canada Cataloguing in Publication

Paré, Jean, date-
Appetizers & snacks / Jean Paré.
(Original series) Includes index.
At head of title: Company's Coming.
ISBN 978-1-897477-46-5
1. Appetizers. 2. Snack foods. I. Title. II. Title:
Appetizers and snacks. III. Series: Paré, Jean, date.
Original series.
TX740.P341 2011   641.8'12   C2010-900562-7

Published by
Company's Coming Publishing Limited
2311 – 96 Street
Edmonton, Alberta, Canada T6N 1G3
Tel: 780-450-6223   Fax: 780-450-1857
www.companyscoming.com

Company's Coming is a registered trademark
owned by Company's Coming Publishing Limited

We acknowledge the financial support of the Government
of Canada through the Canada Book Fund for our
publishing activities.

Printed in China

*We gratefully acknowledge the following
suppliers for their generous support of our
Test and Photography Kitchens:*

Broil King Barbecues
Corelle®
Hamilton Beach® Canada
Lagostina®
Proctor Silex® Canada
Tupperware®

*Our special thanks to the following business
for providing props for photography:*

Ikea
Stokes

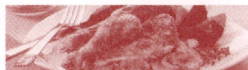

Table of Contents

Entertaining with
Appetizers

Dips & Spreads

Nibbles & Canapés

Rolls, Wraps
& Stacks

Sit-down Starters

Sticks & Skewers

Last-minute Bites

Small Sweets

The Company's Coming Story

Jean Paré (pronounced "jeen PAIR-ee") grew up understanding that the combination of family, friends and home cooking is the best recipe for a good life. From her mother, she learned to appreciate good cooking, while her father praised even her earliest attempts in the kitchen. When Jean left home, she took with her a love of cooking, many family recipes and an intriguing desire to read cookbooks as if they were novels!

"Never share a recipe you wouldn't use yourself."

When her four children had all reached school age, Jean volunteered to cater the 50th anniversary celebration of the Vermilion School of Agriculture, now Lakeland College, in Alberta, Canada. Working out of her home, Jean prepared a dinner for more than 1,000 people, launching a flourishing catering operation that continued for over 18 years. During that time, she had countless opportunities to test new ideas with immediate feedback—resulting in empty plates and contented customers! Whether preparing cocktail sandwiches for a house party or serving a hot meal for 1,500 people, Jean Paré earned a reputation for great food, courteous service and reasonable prices.

As requests for her recipes increased, Jean was often asked the question, "Why don't you write a cookbook?" Jean responded by teaming up with her son, Grant Lovig, in the fall of 1980 to form Company's Coming Publishing Limited. The publication of *150 Delicious Squares* on April 14, 1981 marked the debut of what would soon become one of the world's most popular cookbook series.

The company has grown since those early days when Jean worked from a spare bedroom in her home. Nowadays every Company's Coming recipe is *kitchen-tested* before it is approved for publication.

Company's Coming cookbooks are distributed in Canada, the United States, Australia and other world markets. Bestsellers many times over in English, Company's Coming cookbooks have also been published in French and Spanish.

Familiar and trusted in home kitchens around the world, Company's Coming cookbooks are offered in a variety of formats. Highly regarded as kitchen workbooks, the softcover Original Series, with its lay-flat plastic comb binding, is still a favourite among readers.

Jean Paré's approach to cooking has always called for *quick and easy recipes* using *everyday ingredients*. That view has served her well. The recipient of many awards, including the Queen Elizabeth Golden Jubilee Medal, Jean was appointed Member of the Order of Canada, her country's highest lifetime achievement honour.

Jean continues to share what she calls The Golden Rule of Cooking: *Never share a recipe you wouldn't use yourself.* It's an approach that has worked—*millions of times over!*

Foreword

Whatever you call them—starters, finger foods, hors d'oeuvres, *amuse-bouches*, *antipasti*—appetizers offer great variety and versatility. Whether part of a formal meal or the stars of the show, they are ideal for entertaining. A spread of appetizers and bite-sized snacks not only looks inviting, but also offers guests a tempting range of irresistable little dishes to sample, some of which they may never have tried before. *Appetizers & Snacks* features delicious and approachable starter recipes that use everyday ingredients with flair.

Our Sit-down Starters section is perfect for those occasions when you want just one or two starters to serve at a meal. Recipes include a light and simple Goat Cheese Pecan Salad and Fennel Radicchio Slaw, an adventurous and full-flavoured Spicy Roasted Pepper Soup and Shrimp Ceviche, and the cosy comfort of Tuscan Terrine and Buttery Sage Linguine. There's an appetizer to match practically any dinner menu.

For an entire evening's meal of appetizers, include a few hot and cold dips, such as Layered Antipasto Dip and Hot Crab Dip, along with some nibbles and canapés, like Pesto Mascarpone Bites, Asian Lobster Canapés, Three-cheese Garlic Toasts and Avocado Bacon Triangles. Add to that a selection of rolls, wraps and skewers that could include Lemony Chicken Rolls, Mini Reuben Stacks, California Sushi Skewers, Pork Jicama Lettuce Wraps, Mango Veggie Skewers and Marinated Bocconcini Bites. Finally, cap it all off with Mocha Pots de Crème, Orange Poppy Seed Cupcakes or Chocolate Orange Mousse for a sweet and satifying ending.

Recipes in *Appetizers & Snacks* use fresh ingredients; several, such as Spinach Bean Dip, Keftedes with Dill Yogurt and Raspberry Basil Scallops, will also appeal to the health-conscious guest. You'll also find the Last-minute Bites section helpful for those times when unexpected company pops in. Make sure to try our simple Tortilla Wedges and our stunning Strawberry Brie Canapés—impressive appetizers that come together quickly and easily.

You'll have a great time entertaining with *Appetizers & Snacks*. The only challenge will be in trying to decide which delectable appetizer to make first!

Nutrition Information Guidelines

Each recipe is analyzed using the most current versions of the Canadian Nutrient File from Health Canada, and the United States Department of Agriculture (USDA) Nutrient Database for Standard Reference.

- If more than one ingredient is listed (such as "butter or hard margarine"), or if a range is given (1 – 2 tsp., 5 – 10 mL), only the first ingredient or first amount is analyzed.
- For meat, poultry and fish, the recommended serving size per person is 4 oz. (113 g) uncooked weight (without bone), which is 2 – 3 oz. (57 – 85 g) cooked weight (without bone)—approximately the size of a deck of playing cards.
- Milk used is 1% M.F. (milk fat), unless otherwise stated.
- Cooking oil used is canola oil, unless otherwise stated.
- Ingredients indicating "sprinkle," "optional" or "for garnish" are not included in the nutrition information.
- The fat in recipes and combination foods can vary greatly depending upon the sources and types of fats used in each specific ingredient. For these reasons, the amount of saturated, monounsaturated and polyunsaturated fats may not add up to the total fat content.

Entertaining with Appetizers

These days, the trend in eating and in-home entertaining is more casual than in the past. Providing guests with many small dishes to sample rather than creating one elaborate, formal, multi-course dinner is certainly becoming a more popular option. With changing lifestyles and tastes, more people want to try many different kinds of foods rather than be restricted to a menu of traditional courses. *Appetizers & Snacks* presents a collection of fresh and imaginative recipe ideas, from the classic and traditional to the modern and contemporary, to help you put together an appetizer party that's sure to impress.

Everyday Ingredients

You may be intimidated by the thought of trying to prepare a number of different small dishes, and worry about what it will cost to purchase any expensive ingredients. The beauty of *Appetizers & Snacks* is that all the recipes are made with affordable, everyday ingredients easily found at the local grocery store. This makes for no-hassle shopping and preparation, leaving you plenty of time to mull over which delicious appetizers go best together and match your guests' tastes and preferences.

Something for Everyone

Our recipes cover a wide range of ingredients, flavours and presentation possibilities. We have options for any occasion, including dips and spreads, wraps and rolls, sticks and skewers and even desserts! There's even a section of last-minute ideas for serving to surprise guests! Appetizers can be so versatile that they may present you with a bit of a dilemma—what to serve and how many?

Menu Planning

Planning your appetizer menu will depend on what sort of party you're going to be hosting and how many people will be attending. If you simply need starters before a larger meal, consider the rest of your menu; if you're serving something heavier as a main course, go for light starters such as elegant soups or salads. You can also use appetizers to mirror the style of your party. For a fun outdoor barbecue, for example, present small skewers before the main event.

If you're hosting a cocktail party where only appetizers will be served, include heartier recipes that will satisfy everyone's appetites throughout the night. Vary your selection to include items such as hot dips, fun finger foods and chic canapés to please every palate. Remember to top up any dwindling supplies, and replenish small plates, napkins, toothpicks or finger bowls as necessary.

If you're wondering just how many appetizers you should serve, here are some general guidelines that may help: if your appetizers are served as part of a meal, four to five per person should be enough. If appetizers are the only thing on the menu, plan for 10 or more per person. For an average party crowd of 10 to 20 people, serve a minimum of half a dozen different appetizers, in addition to bowls of snacks such as spiced nuts and crackers, to ensure enough variety and quantity.

Planning Ahead

It really pays to plan ahead as much as possible, especially for a large cocktail party. Depending on the recipes you've selected, you can shop for and prep much of the food in advance. Many recipes in *Appetizers & Snacks* can be made ahead and chilled or frozen, which will help you to get things done in good time. You don't want to leave things to the last minute—it's no fun to be a harried host with barely a moment to enjoy your own party or chat with your guests!

Do as many of the preparations as possible in the days leading up to the party. If you get yourself organized early, you can save the day of the party for doing the fun things, like adding the special touches that guests appreciate, such as creative serving vessels, comfortable seating, cozy lighting, and decorating with vases of flowers.

If you're serving many people in a large space, also plan on setting up several food and beverage stations with an ample supply of food and drink at each one. That way none of your guests has to travel very far to get a tasty snack and beverage.

Food Safety

Always take food safety into account when leaving out appetizers for grazing, and ensure that hot items stay hot and cold items stay cold. For dishes such as hot dips or wings, keep foods at serving temperature with chafing dishes, a slow cooker with a "keep warm" setting or warming trays. Store chilled items, such as those made with seafood, in the fridge until the last minute possible and set them over bowls of ice to keep them cold. Be sure to reserve portions of temperature-sensitive foods in the oven or refrigerator for topping up the dishes.

For any other appetizers, follow the two-hour rule: never allow food to linger on the table for more than two hours. If you have a large amount, simply set out smaller portions and use clean serving dishes for refills. Make your party fare user-friendly! Provide spoons in sauces and dips, and set out tongs so guests don't have to use their hands.

Last-minute Bites

Occasionally, guests may pop in at the last minute, or you may be called upon to entertain on short notice. We've created a Last-minute Bites section to help you through these times. You'll find the recipes in this section are simpler and take less time to prepare. The recipes in Last-minute Bites make use of readily available ingredients, many of which you may already have in your pantry. All the recipes are ready to serve in less than 30 minutes.

To assist with these occasions, we've created a short list of specialty items that you may wish to keep on hand so that you're always prepared:

• Basil pesto

• Brie

• Chili paste (sambal oelek)

• Curry paste

• Flour tortillas

• Ginger marmalade

• Roasted red pepper

• Smoked salmon

Many of these specialty items will last a long time in your fridge or freezer so you won't need to worry about wasting them. Keeping a stock of these ingredients is particularly wise around holidays or the summer barbecue season when you know you'll be doing more entertaining. Add in a few of the usual suspects from your pantry, like crackers, cream cheese, fresh herbs and deli meats, and you'll be able to create a number of quick recipes from Last-minute Bites.

Keep in mind that many of the other recipes in *Appetizers & Snacks* are also easy to put together—if you do get a little advance notice, don't rule out the other great sections we've included!

Appetizers & Snacks will make entertaining so fun and easy, you'll want to host more parties so you can try every recipe!

Spinach Bean Dip

Satisfy a craving for a creamy spinach dip without overindulging. This thick, garlicky dip has lots of contrasting textures, and can be served with raw vegetables, Melba toast or whole-wheat pita bread for dipping.

Can of navy beans, rinsed and drained	19 oz.	540 mL
2% cottage cheese	1 cup	250 mL
Cooking oil	2 tbsp.	30 mL
Lemon juice	2 tbsp.	30 mL
Prepared vegetable broth	2 tbsp.	30 mL
Grated onion	1 tbsp.	15 mL
Garlic cloves, chopped	2	2
(or 1/2 tsp., 2 mL, powder)		
Box of frozen chopped spinach, thawed and squeezed dry	10 oz.	300 g
Can of sliced water chestnuts, drained, chopped	8 oz.	227 mL
Finely chopped red pepper	1/4 cup	60 mL
Grated Parmesan cheese	3 tbsp.	45 mL
Chopped fresh parsley	1 tbsp.	15 mL
(or 3/4 tsp., 4 mL, flakes)		
Pepper	1/4 tsp.	1 mL
Celery salt	1/8 tsp.	0.5 mL
Hot pepper sauce	1/8 tsp.	0.5 mL

Process first 7 ingredients in food processor until smooth and creamy. Transfer to medium bowl.

Add remaining 8 ingredients. Stir. Chill, covered, for 30 minutes to blend flavours. Makes about 4 cups (1 L).

1/4 cup (60 mL): 161 Calories; 3.0 g Total Fat (1.2 g Mono, 0.8 g Poly, 0.5 g Sat); 2 mg Cholesterol; 24 g Carbohydrate; 9 g Fibre; 11 g Protein; 139 mg Sodium

tip The microwaves used in our test kitchen are 900 watts—but microwaves are sold in many different powers. You should be able to find the wattage of yours by opening the door and looking for the mandatory label. If your microwave is more than 900 watts, you may need to reduce the cooking time. If it's less than 900 watts, you'll probably need to increase the cooking time.

Artichoke Salmon Pâté

Lemon brightens up this classic pairing of salmon, artichokes and goat cheese.
Baguette toasts, rye crisps or water crackers are well suited for this pâté.

Jar of marinated artichoke hearts, drained, finely chopped	6 oz.	170 mL
Soft goat (chèvre) cheese	5 oz.	140 g
Finely chopped smoked salmon (about 1 1/4 oz., 35 g)	1/4 cup	60 mL
Chopped fresh parsley	2 tbsp.	30 mL
Lemon juice	2 tsp.	10 mL
Chopped fresh dill	1/2 tsp.	2 mL
Coarsely ground pepper	1/4 tsp.	1 mL

Combine all 7 ingredients in small microwave-safe bowl. Microwave, covered, on medium for about 45 seconds until just warmed through (see Tip, page 11). Serve immediately. Makes about 1 1/3 cups (325 mL).

1/4 cup (60 mL): 91 Calories; 5.8 g Total Fat (1.4 g Mono, 0.2 g Poly, 3.9 g Sat); 14 mg Cholesterol; 3 g Carbohydrate; trace Fibre; 7 g Protein; 228 mg Sodium

Apricot Blue Cheese Spread

Bold blue cheese pairs with walnuts and sweet apricot in this attractive layered spread, best served with pumpernickel points and Granny Smith apple slices. Make sure your choice of mold is not too wide and fairly deep to make the layers more defined.

Block cream cheese, softened	4 oz.	125 g
Finely chopped dried apricot	1/4 cup	60 mL
Chopped walnuts, toasted (see Tip, page 77)	1/4 cup	60 mL
Block cream cheese, softened	4 oz.	125 g
Blue cheese, crumbled	2 oz.	57 g
Chopped fresh basil (or 3/4 tsp., 4 mL, dried)	1 tbsp.	15 mL
Chopped fresh chives (or green onion)	1 tbsp.	15 mL

(continued on next page)

Dips & Spreads

Line greased 1 1/2 cup (375 mL) mold or small bowl with plastic wrap. Combine first amount of cream cheese and apricot in small bowl. Press into prepared mold.

Scatter walnuts over top. Press down lightly.

Combine next 4 ingredients in same small bowl. Spoon over walnuts. Press into even layer. Chill, covered, for at least 4 hours until firm. Invert onto serving plate. Discard plastic wrap. Makes about 1 1/2 cups (375 mL).

2 tbsp. (30 mL): 102 Calories; 9.2 g Total Fat (2.4 g Mono, 1.4 g Poly, 5.0 g Sat); 23 mg Cholesterol; 3 g Carbohydrate; trace Fibre; 3 g Protein; 119 mg Sodium

---

Guacamole Mousse

This smooth, creamy and elegant avocado mousse is perfect for serving with tortilla chips.

Water	1/2 cup	125 mL
Granulated sugar	2 tsp.	10 mL
Envelope of unflavoured gelatin (about 2 1/4 tsp., 11 mL)	1/4 oz.	7 g
Mashed avocado	1 cup	250 mL
Sour cream	1/2 cup	125 mL
Lemon juice	1/4 cup	60 mL
Salt	1/2 tsp.	2 mL
Whipping cream	1/2 cup	125 mL

Combine water and sugar in small saucepan. Sprinkle gelatin over top. Let stand for 1 minute. Heat and stir on low until gelatin is dissolved. Cool to room temperature.

Beat next 4 ingredients in medium bowl until smooth. Whisk in gelatin mixture. Let stand for 2 minutes until starting to thicken.

Beat whipping cream in small bowl until stiff peaks form. Fold into avocado mixture until combined. Spread evenly in 4 cup (1 L) serving bowl. Chill, covered, for about 1 hour until set. Makes about 3 cups (750 mL).

1/4 cup (60 mL): 90 Calories; 8.2 g Total Fat (2.9 g Mono, 0.5 g Poly, 3.9 g Sat); 20 mg Cholesterol; 3 g Carbohydrate; 1 g Fibre; 1 g Protein; 107 mg Sodium

Red Lentil Cashew Pâté

A smooth, thick and nutty spread with a hummus-like texture—best served with crackers and fresh vegetables.

Prepared chicken broth	2 cups	500 mL
Bay leaf	1	1
Dried red split lentils	1 cup	250 mL
Unsalted, roasted cashews	1 cup	250 mL
Chopped onion	2 tbsp.	30 mL
Mayonnaise	2 tbsp.	30 mL
Cooking oil	1 tbsp.	15 mL
Dijon mustard	2 tsp.	10 mL
Ground cumin	1/2 tsp.	2 mL
Paprika	1/2 tsp.	2 mL
Pepper	1/2 tsp.	2 mL
Celery salt	1/8 tsp.	0.5 mL
Large hard-cooked eggs, halved (see Tip, below)	2	2
Paprika, for garnish		

Combine broth and bay leaf in small saucepan. Bring to a boil. Add lentils. Stir. Reduce heat to medium-low. Simmer, covered, for about 25 minutes until lentils are tender and broth is absorbed. Discard bay leaf. Cool.

Process cashews in food processor until coarsely ground.

Add next 8 ingredients. Process until mixture resembles paste.

Add eggs and lentils. Process until smooth. Press into plastic wrap-lined 4 cup (1 L) mold or small bowl. Chill, covered, for 6 hours or overnight until firm. Invert onto serving plate. Discard plastic wrap.

Sprinkle with paprika. Makes about 3 1/2 cups (875 mL).

1/4 cup (60 mL): 146 Calories; 8.4 g Total Fat (3.6 g Mono, 1.2 g Poly, 1.5 g Sat); 31 mg Cholesterol; 12 g Carbohydrate; 2 g Fibre; 7 g Protein; 152 mg Sodium

tip To make hard-cooked eggs, place eggs in a single layer in a saucepan. Add cold water until it's about 1 inch (2.5 cm) above the eggs. Bring to a boil, covered. Reduce heat to medium-low. Simmer for 10 minutes. Drain. Cover the eggs with cold water. Change the water each time it warms until the eggs are cool enough to handle. Remove the shells.

Dips & Spreads

Blueberry Fruit Dip

A tangy blueberry dip that's super simple to whip up—a not-too-sweet option for a wedding shower or baby shower. Serve with fresh sliced apple, banana, mango, melon, pineapple and strawberries for dipping. This can be made a few hours before serving.

Block cream cheese, softened	8 oz.	250 g
Fresh (or frozen, thawed) blueberries	1 cup	250 mL
Plain yogurt	1/2 cup	125 mL
Brown sugar, packed	1/4 cup	60 mL
Flaked coconut	1/4 cup	60 mL

Process all 5 ingredients in food processor until smooth. Makes about 2 1/3 cups (575 mL).

1/4 cup (60 mL): 129 Calories; 9.5 g Total Fat (2.4 g Mono, 0.3 g Poly, 6.3 g Sat); 26 mg Cholesterol; 9 g Carbohydrate; 1 g Fibre; 3 g Protein; 83 mg Sodium

Pictured on page 18.

Beautiful Beet Dip

Unique in appearance and surprising in flavour—you may expect sweetness, but this dip has a savoury beet and fresh dill flavour instead. A fun change from the usual that goes great with pita chips or fresh veggies. Garnish with a dollop of sour cream and a sprig of fresh dill.

Round butter-flavoured crackers	15	15
Can of sliced beets, drained	14 oz.	398 mL
Sour cream	1/4 cup	60 mL
Orange juice	1 tbsp.	15 mL
Chopped fresh dill (or 3/4 tsp., 4 mL, dried)	2 tsp.	10 mL
Liquid honey	2 tsp.	10 mL
Dijon mustard	1/2 tsp.	2 mL
Salt	1/8 tsp.	0.5 mL

Process crackers in food processor until fine crumbs.

Add remaining 7 ingredients. Process until smooth. Chill, covered, for 1 hour to blend flavours. Makes about 1 1/4 cups (300 mL).

1/4 cup (60 mL): 96 Calories; 3.7 g Total Fat (trace Mono, trace Poly, 2.0 g Sat); 13 mg Cholesterol; 14 g Carbohydrate; 1 g Fibre; 2 g Protein; 273 mg Sodium

Garden-fresh Salsa

This colourful, fresh and healthy-tasting salsa is a great make-ahead option that can be refrigerated overnight—serve it with plenty of tortilla chips! Use the leftover black beans in a soup or salad.

Canned black beans, rinsed and drained	1 cup	250 mL
Diced tomato, seeds removed	1 cup	250 mL
Diced zucchini (with peel)	2/3 cup	150 mL
Fresh (or frozen) kernel corn	2/3 cup	150 mL
Salsa	1/2 cup	125 mL
Grated carrot	1/3 cup	75 mL
Chopped green onion	1/4 cup	60 mL
Chopped fresh cilantro (or parsley)	2 tbsp.	30 mL
Lime juice	1 tbsp.	15 mL
Chili powder	1 tsp.	5 mL
Grated lime zest (see Tip, page 93)	1/2 tsp.	2 mL
Ground cumin	1/2 tsp.	2 mL
Salt	1/2 tsp.	2 mL

Combine all 13 ingredients in medium bowl. Let stand, covered, for 2 hours, stirring occasionally, to blend flavours. Makes about 3 cups (750 mL).

1/4 cup (60 mL): 35 Calories; 0.3 g Total Fat (trace Mono, 0.2 g Poly, trace Sat); 0 mg Cholesterol; 6 g Carbohydrate; 2 g Fibre; 2 g Protein; 206 mg Sodium

Pictured at right.

1. Quick Red Pepper Guacamole, page 134
2. Garden-fresh Salsa, above
3. Margarita Shrimp, page 115

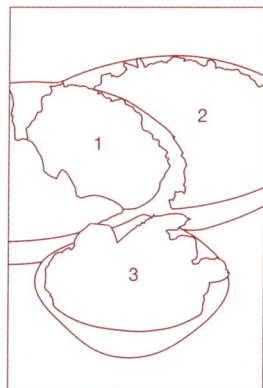

Cucumber Mango Salsa

Sweet mango combines with crunchy cucumber and red onion in this mildly spicy salsa. It pairs perfectly with tortilla chips or toasted pita wedges, and also makes an elegant condiment for grilled fish. Even made the day before, it will remain fresh and crunchy.

Diced fresh (or frozen, thawed) mango	1 1/2 cups	375 mL
Diced English cucumber (with peel)	1 cup	250 mL
Finely chopped red onion	1/4 cup	60 mL
Lime juice	3 tbsp.	45 mL
Chopped fresh cilantro (or parsley)	2 tbsp.	30 mL
Olive (or cooking) oil	2 tbsp.	30 mL
Finely chopped fresh jalapeño pepper (see Tip, page 115)	2 tsp.	10 mL
Salt	1/8 tsp.	0.5 mL

Combine all 8 ingredients in medium bowl. Chill, covered, for 2 hours to blend flavours. Makes about 2 cups (500 mL).

1/4 cup (60 mL): 57 Calories; 3.6 g Total Fat (2.7 g Mono, 0.3 g Poly, 0.5 g Sat); 7 mg Cholesterol; 7 g Carbohydrate; 1 g Fibre; trace Protein; 38 mg Sodium

Pictured at left.

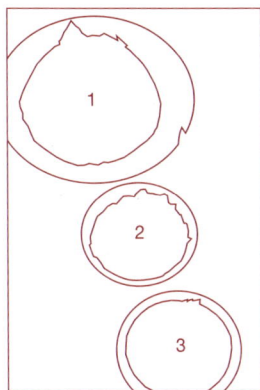

1. Smoked Salmon Artichoke Dip, page 28
2. Cucumber Mango Salsa, above
3. Blueberry Fruit Dip, page 15
Props: Ikea

Fiesta Dip

This thick and creamy dip has a smooth tomato flavour and a kick of chipotle spice. Fresh bites of tomato and cilantro create an addictive party dip to serve with vegetables.

Envelope of tomato vegetable soup mix (2.5 oz., 71 g), stir before dividing	1/2	1/2
Sour cream	1 1/2 cups	375 mL
Mayonnaise	1/2 cup	125 mL
Lime juice	1 1/2 tsp.	7 mL
Chopped chipotle peppers in adobo sauce (see Tip, page 97)	1/2 tsp.	2 mL
Chopped tomato, seeds removed	3/4 cup	175 mL
Chopped fresh cilantro (or parsley)	1 tbsp.	15 mL

Process soup mix in blender or food processor until finely ground. Add next 4 ingredients. Process until smooth. Transfer to medium bowl.

Add tomato and cilantro. Stir. Chill, covered, for 1 hour to blend flavours. Makes about 2 3/4 cups (675 mL).

1/4 cup (60 mL): 151 Calories; 13.7 g Total Fat (trace Mono, trace Poly, 5.0 g Sat); 26 mg Cholesterol; 4 g Carbohydrate; 14 g Fibre; 2 g Protein; 284 mg Sodium

Spiced Carrot Dip

A vibrantly coloured carrot dip that's creamy and tangy with a bit of chili spice—and it's low-fat to boot! Serve with pita chips, toasted flatbread, wheat crackers or fresh veggies.

Coarsely chopped carrot	2 cups	500 mL
Sour cream	1/2 cup	125 mL
Ginger marmalade	2 tbsp.	30 mL
Lime juice	2 tbsp.	30 mL
Chili paste (sambal oelek)	1/2 tsp.	2 mL
Curry powder	1/2 tsp.	2 mL
Granulated sugar	1/2 tsp.	2 mL
Salt	1/8 tsp.	0.5 mL

(continued on next page)

Dips & Spreads

Pour water into medium saucepan until about 1 inch (2.5 cm) deep. Add carrot. Cover. Bring to a boil. Reduce heat to medium. Boil gently for about 15 minutes until soft. Drain, reserving 2 tbsp. (30 mL) cooking liquid in small cup. Transfer to food processor.

Add remaining 7 ingredients and reserved cooking liquid. Process until smooth. Makes about 1 3/4 cups (425 mL).

1/4 cup (60 mL): 66 Calories; 3.0 g Total Fat (trace Mono, 0.1 Poly, 2.0 g Sat); 11 mg Cholesterol; 9 g Carbohydrate; 1 g Fibre; 1 g Protein; 83 mg Sodium

Hot Crab Dip

Hot dips are always among the first appetizers to disappear! This one has an appealing paprika-speckled topping over a rich, cheesy dip with sweet crab and bacon. Serve with crackers or Melba toast and fresh celery sticks.

Chopped seeded tomato	3/4 cup	175 mL
Sour cream	3/4 cup	175 mL
Can of crabmeat, drained, cartilage removed, flaked	6 oz.	170 g
Mayonnaise	1/2 cup	125 mL
Goat (chèvre) cheese, cut up	4 oz.	113 g
Finely chopped onion	3 tbsp.	45 mL
Bacon slices, cooked crisp and crumbled	2	2
Chopped fresh basil (or 3/4 tsp., 4 mL, dried)	1 tbsp.	15 mL
Dijon mustard	1 tsp.	5 mL
White wine vinegar	1 tsp.	5 mL
Coarsely ground pepper	1/2 tsp.	2 mL
Tabasco sauce	1/8 tsp.	0.5 mL
Fine dry bread crumbs	2 tbsp.	30 mL
Ground almonds	1 tbsp.	15 mL
Paprika	1/4 tsp.	1 mL

Combine first 12 ingredients in medium bowl. Spread evenly in ungreased 9 inch (23 cm) deep dish pie plate.

Combine remaining 3 ingredients in small cup. Sprinkle over crab mixture. Bake in 350°F (175°C) oven for about 30 minutes until top is golden and crab mixture is bubbling. Makes about 3 cups (750 mL).

1/4 cup (60 mL): 162 Calories; 13.6 g Total Fat (1.0 g Mono, 0.3 g Poly, 4.9 g Sat); 35 mg Cholesterol; 2 g Carbohydrate; trace Fibre; 6 g Protein; 190 mg Sodium

Dips & Spreads

Layered Antipasto Dip

Tasty antipasto flavours are a nice departure from your ordinary layered dip.
Serve this hearty dip with sturdy pita crisps or crackers.

Olive (or cooking) oil	1 tsp.	5 mL
Lean ground beef	1/2 lb.	225 g
Dried oregano	1/2 tsp.	2 mL
Garlic clove, minced	1	1
(or 1/4 tsp., 1 mL, powder)		
Roasted red pepper hummus	1 cup	250 mL
Can of sliced black olives, drained	4 1/2 oz.	125 mL
Diced green pepper	1/4 cup	60 mL
Diced tomato	1/4 cup	60 mL
Roasted red peppers, blotted dry, diced	1/4 cup	60 mL
Sliced green onion	1/4 cup	60 mL
Olive (or cooking) oil	3 tbsp.	45 mL
Red wine vinegar	2 tbsp.	30 mL
Sun-dried tomatoes in oil,	2 tbsp.	30 mL
blotted dry, finely chopped		
Water	2 tbsp.	30 mL
Granulated sugar	1 tsp.	5 mL
Crumbled feta cheese	1 cup	250 mL
Sliced green onion	2 tbsp.	30 mL

Heat first amount of olive oil in medium frying pan on medium. Add next 3 ingredients. Scramble-fry for about 10 minutes until beef is no longer pink. Transfer to paper towel-lined plate to drain. Cool.

Spread hummus evenly in ungreased 9 inch (23 cm) pie plate. Scatter beef mixture over hummus.

Combine next 5 ingredients in medium bowl.

Process next 5 ingredients in blender or food processor until smooth. Drizzle over olive mixture. Toss until coated. Scatter over beef mixture. Press down lightly.

Sprinkle with cheese and green onion. Chill. Makes about 4 cups (1 L).

1/4 cup (60 mL): 118 Calories; 9.1 g Total Fat (3.27 g Mono, 0.4 g Poly, 2.8 g Sat); 18 mg Cholesterol; 4 g Carbohydrate; 1 g Fibre; 5 g Protein; 281 mg Sodium

Dips & Spreads

Roasted Pepper Antipasto

Classic antipasto flavour with added colour and flavour from a blend of bell peppers. Serve it up with Melba toast or pita chips.

Medium red pepper, halved	1	1
Medium orange pepper, halved	1	1
Medium yellow pepper, halved	1	1
Salsa	3 cups	750 mL
Can of flaked light tuna in water, drained	6 oz.	170 mL
Jar of marinated artichoke hearts, drained, chopped	6 oz.	170 mL
Sliced green olives, chopped	1/2 cup	125 mL
Finely chopped pickled onions	1/4 cup	60 mL
Chopped fresh parsley (or 1 1/2 tsp., 7 mL, flakes)	2 tbsp.	30 mL
Lemon juice	1 tbsp.	15 mL
Coarsely ground pepper	1/4 tsp.	1 mL
Garlic clove, minced (or 1/4 tsp., 1 mL, powder)	1	1

Arrange red, orange and yellow pepper halves, cut-side down, on greased baking sheet with sides. Broil on top rack in oven for about 10 minutes until skins are blistered and blackened. Transfer to medium bowl. Cover with plastic wrap. Let stand for about 15 minutes until cool enough to handle. Remove and discard skins. Chop. Transfer to medium bowl.

Add remaining 9 ingredients. Stir. Chill, covered, for 2 hours to blend flavours. Makes about 5 cups (1.25 L).

1/4 cup (60 mL): 38 Calories; 1.0 g Total Fat (0.6 g Mono, 0.2 g Poly, 0.2 g Sat); 4 mg Cholesterol; 4 g Carbohydrate; trace Fibre; 2 g Protein; 258 mg Sodium

Avocado Feta Salsa

A tasty salsa reminiscent of guacamole. Enjoy the delicious balance of the bright, fresh flavours of garlic, cilantro, tomato and feta. Serve with tortilla chips or wheat crackers.

Chopped Roma (plum) tomato, seeds removed	2 cups	500 mL
Chopped avocado	1 1/2 cups	375 mL
Finely chopped red onion	2 tbsp.	30 mL
White wine vinegar	2 tbsp.	30 mL
Chopped fresh cilantro	1 tbsp.	15 mL
Chopped fresh parsley	1 tbsp.	15 mL
Garlic clove, minced (or 1/4 tsp., 1 mL, powder)	1	1
Crumbled feta cheese	3/4 cup	175 mL

Combine first 7 ingredients in large bowl. Chill, covered, for 2 hours.

Add cheese. Stir gently. Makes about 3 1/2 cups (875 mL).

1/4 cup (60 mL): 52 Calories; 4.1 g Total Fat (2.0 g Mono, 0.4 g Poly, 1.6 g Sat); 7 mg Cholesterol; 3 g Carbohydrate; 1 g Fibre; 2 g Protein; 92 mg Sodium

Sesame Seed Hummus

Thick, lemony and garlicky—just like good hummus should be! It's delicious with your favourite dippers, or spread onto sandwiches.

Can of chickpeas (garbanzo beans), rinsed and drained	19 oz.	540 mL
Olive (or cooking) oil	1/4 cup	60 mL
Lemon juice	2 tbsp.	30 mL
Roasted sesame seeds	2 tbsp.	30 mL
Chopped fresh parsley (or 3/4 tsp., 4 mL, flakes)	1 tbsp.	15 mL
Garlic cloves, chopped (or 1/2 tsp., 2 mL, powder)	2	2
Salt	1/2 tsp.	2 mL
Pepper	1/4 tsp.	1 mL

(continued on next page)

Dips & Spreads

Process all 8 ingredients in food processor until smooth. Makes about 1 3/4 cups (425 mL).

1/4 cup (60 mL): 157 Calories; 10.4 g Total Fat (6.5 g Mono, 1.3 g Poly, 1.1 g Sat); 0 mg Cholesterol; 12 g Carbohydrate; 3 g Fibre; 4 g Protein; 249 mg Sodium

Roasted Leek Butter

A tangy and mildly sweet dip that's perfectly paired with Pepper Rye Points for dipping—a combination that's made for sharing!

ROASTED LEEK BUTTER

Chopped leek (white part only)	8 cups	2 L
Cooking oil	2 tbsp.	30 mL
Garlic clove, halved	1	1
Rice vinegar	2 tbsp.	30 mL
Cooking oil	1 tbsp.	15 mL
Dijon mustard (with whole seeds)	2 tsp.	10 mL
Brown sugar, packed	1 tsp.	5 mL
Finely grated ginger root	1 tsp.	5 mL
(or 1/4 tsp., 1 mL, ground ginger)		
Salt	1/2 tsp.	2 mL
Coarsely ground pepper, sprinkle		

PEPPER RYE POINTS

Butter (or hard margarine), melted	2 tbsp.	30 mL
Light rye bread slices, crusts removed	9	9
Coarsely ground pepper, sprinkle		

Roasted Leek Butter: Toss first 3 ingredients in large bowl until coated. Arrange on large baking sheet with sides. Cook in 375°F (190°C) oven for about 40 minutes, stirring occasionally, until leeks are golden. Cool slightly. Transfer to food processor.

Add next 7 ingredients. Process until smooth. Pack into small bowl. Makes about 1 1/3 cups (325 mL).

Pepper Rye Points: Brush butter over bread slices. Sprinkle with pepper. Cut each slice diagonally into 2 triangles. Arrange on greased baking sheet. Bake in 375°F (190°C) oven for about 15 minutes until golden. Serve with Roasted Leek Butter. Makes 18 toast points.

1 toast point with 1 tbsp. (15 mL) leek butter: 77 Calories; 3.3 g Total Fat (1.4 g Mono, 0.7 g Poly, 0.8 g Sat); 3 mg Cholesterol; 10 g Carbohydrate; 2 g Fibre; 2 g Protein; 106 mg Sodium

Salmon Mousse

*This classic mousse is highlighted with the fresh tastes of dill and lemon.
Serve it with rye, pumpernickel or French bread.*

Envelope of unflavoured gelatin (about 2 1/4 tsp., 11 mL)	1/4 oz.	7 g
Water	1/4 cup	60 mL
Can of red salmon, drained, skin and round bones removed	7 1/2 oz.	213 g
Sour cream	3/4 cup	175 mL
Chopped fresh dill (or 1 1/2 tsp., 7 mL, dried)	2 tbsp.	30 mL
Lemon juice	1 tbsp.	15 mL
Minced onion	1 tbsp.	15 mL
Paprika	1/2 tsp.	2 mL
Salt	1/4 tsp.	1 mL
Whipping cream	1/4 cup	60 mL

Sprinkle gelatin over water in small saucepan. Let stand for 1 minute. Heat and stir on low until gelatin is dissolved. Cool to room temperature.

Beat next 7 ingredients in medium bowl until smooth. Add gelatin mixture. Stir.

Beat whipping cream in small bowl until stiff peaks form. Fold into salmon mixture until combined. Spoon into greased 2 cup (500 mL) mold. Chill, covered, for about 2 hours until firm. Invert onto serving plate, shaking gently to release. Makes about 2 cups (500 mL).

1/4 cup (60 mL): 94 Calories; 5.5 g Total Fat (0 g Mono, trace Poly, 3.2 g Sat); 37 mg Cholesterol; 2 g Carbohydrate; trace Fibre; 8 g Protein; 178 mg Sodium

Whipped Mango Butter

A pretty pastel spread that goes well with crackers or cocktail bread slices for a satisfying snack. The lime and mango come through nicely without being overpowering.

Butter, softened	1/2 cup	125 mL
Finely chopped fresh (or frozen, thawed) mango	1/4 cup	60 mL
Liquid honey	1 tsp.	5 mL
Grated lime zest	1/2 tsp.	2 mL

Beat all 4 ingredients in medium bowl until light and creamy. Makes about 2/3 cup (150 mL).

1 tbsp. (15 mL): 85 Calories; 9.1 g Total Fat (2.4 g Mono, 0.3 g Poly, 5.8 g Sat); 24 mg Cholesterol; 1 g Carbohydrate; trace Fibre; trace Protein; 65 mg Sodium

Mediterranean Dip

Tangy yogurt dip blended with bold Mediterranean flavours—it's fresh and flavourful with garlic, lemon and feta. Serve with pita bread and chips or wheat crackers.

Plain Balkan-style yogurt	1 cup	250 mL
Crumbled feta cheese	1/2 cup	125 mL
Chopped fresh parsley (or 2 tsp., 10 mL, flakes)	1/4 cup	60 mL
Chopped pitted kalamata olives	2 tbsp.	30 mL
Chopped sliced green olives	2 tbsp.	30 mL
Finely chopped red onion	2 tbsp.	30 mL
Finely chopped red pepper	2 tbsp.	30 mL
Sun-dried tomato pesto	1 tbsp.	15 mL
Grated lemon zest	1/2 tsp.	2 mL
Coarsely ground pepper	1/4 tsp.	1 mL
Garlic powder	1/8 tsp.	0.5 mL

Combine all 11 ingredients in small bowl. Chill, covered, for 1 hour to blend flavours. Makes about 1 3/4 cups (425 mL).

1/4 cup (60 mL): 59 Calories; 3.1 g Total Fat (1.1 g Mono, 0.2 g Poly, 1.6 g Sat); 10 mg Cholesterol; 4 g Carbohydrate; trace Fibre; 4 g Protein; 253 mg Sodium

Smoked Salmon Artichoke Dip

Attractively topped with smoked salmon slices and basil leaves, this dip has delicious layers of flavour. Surround it with a rainbow of fresh vegetables for dipping.

Can of artichoke hearts, drained	14 oz.	398 mL
Herb and garlic cream cheese, softened	8 oz.	250 g
Chopped fresh chives	1 tbsp.	15 mL
Chopped fresh dill	1 tbsp.	15 mL
Grated lemon zest	1 tsp.	5 mL
Chopped smoked salmon slices (about 3 oz., 85 g)	2/3 cup	150 mL
Arugula, lightly packed	1 cup	250 mL
Fresh basil leaves, lightly packed	1/4 cup	60 mL
Smoked salmon slices, cut into 1 inch (2.5 cm) strips (about 3/4 oz., 21 g)	2	2
Fresh basil leaves	5	5

Process first 5 ingredients in food processor until smooth. Reserve 1 cup (250 mL).

Add first amount of salmon to cream cheese mixture in food processor. Process until well combined. Transfer to small bowl.

Combine arugula, basil and reserved cream cheese mixture in food processor. Process until smooth.

Arrange second amounts of smoked salmon and basil in decorative pattern in bottom of plastic wrap-lined 2 1/2 cup (625 mL) mold or bowl. Press half of salmon mixture into bowl. Spread half of arugula mixture evenly over salmon mixture. Repeat with remaining salmon and arugula mixtures. Chill, covered, for about 2 hours until firm. Invert onto serving plate. Discard plastic wrap. Makes about 2 1/3 cups (575 mL).

2 tbsp. (30 mL): 52 Calories; 4.0 g Total Fat (0.1 g Mono, 0.1 g Poly, 2.5 g Sat); 17 mg Cholesterol; 2 g Carbohydrate; trace Fibre; 2 g Protein; 168 mg Sodium

Pictured on page 18.

Dips & Spreads

Chorizo Chili Dip

A hearty chili dip with fresh lime and cilantro flavours, yet it's also rich with tomatoes, black beans and chorizo sausage. Best served hot with tortilla chips, pita chips or crackers.

Chorizo (or hot Italian) sausage, casing removed	1/2 lb.	225 g
Chopped onion	1 cup	250 mL
Chopped celery	1/2 cup	125 mL
Garlic clove, minced (or 1/4 tsp., 1 mL, powder)	1	1
Can of black beans, rinsed and drained	19 oz.	540 mL
Can of diced tomatoes (with juice)	14 oz.	398 mL
Tomato paste (see Tip, page 111)	2 tbsp.	30 mL
Granulated sugar	1/2 tsp.	2 mL
Salt, sprinkle		
Pepper, sprinkle		
Chopped fresh cilantro (or parsley)	1 tbsp.	15 mL
Lime juice	1 tbsp.	15 mL

Scramble-fry sausage in large saucepan on medium for about 8 minutes until browned. Drain.

Add next 3 ingredients. Cook for about 8 minutes, stirring often, until onion and celery are softened.

Add next 6 ingredients. Stir. Bring to a boil. Reduce heat to medium-low. Simmer, covered, for 15 minutes, stirring occasionally, to blend flavours.

Add cilantro and lime. Stir. Makes about 4 cups (1 L).

1/4 cup (60 mL): 90 Calories; 4.2 g Total Fat (1.7 g Mono, 0.7 g Poly, 1.4 g Sat); 8 mg Cholesterol; 8 g Carbohydrate; 2 g Fibre; 5 g Protein; 337 mg Sodium

Fresh Corn Salsa

A confetti-like corn salsa with lots of great texture from sweet corn kernels and summery tomatoes. This healthier choice is bursting with fresh flavour to pair with baked corn chips or crackers, or Greek-style pita breads. Increase the hot pepper sauce if you wish.

Cooking oil	2 tbsp.	30 mL
Lime juice	1 tbsp.	15 mL
Liquid honey	1 tbsp.	15 mL
Garlic clove, minced	1	1
(or 1/4 tsp., 1 mL, powder)		
Hot pepper sauce	1/4 tsp.	1 mL
Salt	1/8 tsp.	0.5 mL
Fresh corn kernels (about	2 cups	500 mL
3 medium cobs)		
Diced Roma (plum) tomato,	1 cup	250 mL
seeds removed		
Diced orange (or red) pepper	1/2 cup	125 mL
Chopped fresh basil	1/4 cup	60 mL
Chopped fresh cilantro (or parsley)	1/4 cup	60 mL
Diced red onion	1/4 cup	60 mL

Whisk first 6 ingredients in large bowl.

Add remaining 6 ingredients. Toss until coated. Let stand for 30 minutes to blend flavours. Makes about 3 1/4 cups (800 mL).

1/4 cup (60 mL): 51 Calories; 2.5 g Total Fat (1.4 g Mono, 0.8 g Poly, 0.2 g Sat); 0 mg Cholesterol; 7 g Carbohydrate; 1 g Fibre; 1 g Protein; 29 mg Sodium

Dips & Spreads

Keftedes with Dill Yogurt

A better-for-you option that's superbly Greek! These keftedes (pronounced kef-TEH-dez) are tender meatballs with a hint of allspice and mint.

DILL YOGURT

Non-fat plain yogurt	2/3 cup	150 mL
Chopped fresh dill	2 tsp.	10 mL
(or 1/2 tsp., 2 mL, dried dill)		
Ground cumin	1/8 tsp.	0.5 mL

KEFTEDES

Large egg, fork-beaten	1	1
Whole-wheat bread slices, processed into crumbs	2	2
Finely chopped onion	1/4 cup	60 mL
Chopped fresh parsley	3 tbsp.	45 mL
(or 2 1/4 tsp., 11 mL, flakes)		
Balsamic vinegar	1 tbsp.	15 mL
Chopped fresh mint leaves	1 tsp.	5 mL
(or 1/4 tsp., 1 mL, dried)		
Ground allspice	1/2 tsp.	2 mL
Garlic clove, minced	1	1
(or 1/4 tsp., 1 mL, powder)		
Salt	1/4 tsp.	1 mL
Pepper	1/4 tsp.	1 mL
Lean ground beef	1 lb.	454 g

Dill Yogurt: Combine all 3 ingredients in small bowl. Chill. Makes about 2/3 cup (150 mL).

Keftedes: Combine first 10 ingredients in large bowl.

Add beef. Mix well. Chill, covered, for 1 hour. Roll into 1 inch (2.5 cm) balls. Arrange in single layer on greased baking sheet with sides. Broil on top rack in oven for about 12 minutes until no longer pink inside. Transfer to serving bowl. Serve with Dill Yogurt. Makes about 36 keftedes.

1 keftede with 1 tsp. (5 mL) yogurt: 36 Calories; 2.1 g Total Fat (0.1 g Mono, trace Poly, 0.8 g Sat); 15 mg Cholesterol; 1 g Carbohydrate; trace Fibre; 3 g Protein; 38 mg Sodium

Salmon Cucumber Cups

Fresh cucumber cups are filled with a spicy salmon mix for a unique and appealing look. The crisp cup nicely balances the creamy filling.

Can of pink salmon, drained, skin and round bones removed	7 1/2 oz.	213 g
Finely chopped red pepper	1/4 cup	60 mL
Mayonnaise	1/4 cup	60 mL
Finely chopped green onion	2 tbsp.	30 mL
Chili paste (sambal oelek)	1 1/2 tsp.	7 mL
Grated lemon zest	1/2 tsp.	2 mL
Salt, sprinkle		
Pepper, sprinkle		
English cucumber slices (with peel), about 3/4 inch (2 cm) each	20	20

Combine first 8 ingredients in small bowl.

Scoop out seeds and flesh from centre of each cucumber slice to make cups. Fill with salmon mixture. Makes 20 salmon cups.

1 salmon cup: 38 Calories; 3.1 g Total Fat (0 g Mono, trace Poly, 0.5 g Sat); 8 mg Cholesterol; 1 g Carbohydrate; trace Fibre; 2 g Protein; 69 mg Sodium

Pictured on page 54.

Grape Pistachio Bites

These miniature cheese balls are an elegant nibble to accompany wine or pre-dinner cocktails—each one has a delightfully sweet grape inside. Choose small grapes and chill well before serving for best results.

Block cream cheese, softened	8 oz.	250 g
Crumbled feta cheese	1/4 cup	60 mL
Chopped fresh chives	2 tbsp.	30 mL
Grated lemon zest	2 tsp.	10 mL
Dried crushed chilies	1/4 tsp.	1 mL
Red or green seedless grapes, patted dry	24	24

(continued on next page)

Nibbles & Canapés

Finely chopped pistachios, toasted (see Tip, page 77)	1 cup	250 mL

Stir first 5 ingredients in medium bowl until smooth.

Spoon cream cheese mixture, in twenty-four 1 tbsp. (15 mL) portions, onto waxed paper-lined baking sheet with sides. Press 1 grape into each portion. With damp hands, roll into balls, enclosing grapes.

Put pistachios into medium shallow bowl. Roll balls in pistachios until coated. Chill for at least 1 hour. Makes 24 bites.

1 bite: 71 Calories; 6.1 g Total Fat (2.3 g Mono, 0.9 g Poly, 2.6 g Sat); 12 mg Cholesterol; 3 g Carbohydrate; 1 g Fibre; 2 g Protein; 67 mg Sodium

Pictured on page 53 and on back cover.

Tomato Basil Shortbread

These shortbread coins have a delicious savoury flavour with bites of sun-dried tomato. They're perfect served with wine and cheese. These will store in airtight containers in the freezer for up to two months.

Butter, softened	3/4 cup	175 mL
Sun-dried tomato pesto	1 tbsp.	15 mL
Icing (confectioner's) sugar	1/4 cup	60 mL
All-purpose flour	1 1/3 cups	325 mL
Finely chopped fresh basil (or 3/4 tsp., 4 mL, dried)	1 tbsp.	15 mL
Salt	1/8 tsp.	0.5 mL

Beat butter and pesto in medium bowl until combined.

Add sugar. Beat until light and fluffy.

Add remaining 3 ingredients. Stir until no dry flour remains. Roll into 12 inch (30 cm) long log. Wrap with plastic wrap. Chill for about 1 hour until firm. Discard plastic wrap. Cut into 1/4 inch (6 mm) slices. Arrange, about 1 inch (2.5 cm) apart, on greased cookie sheets. Bake in 300°F (150°C) oven for about 15 minutes until edges are golden. Let stand on cookie sheets for 5 minutes before removing to wire racks to cool. Makes about 44 cookies.

1 cookie: 42 Calories; 3.1 g Total Fat (0.8 g Mono, 0.1 g Poly, 2.0 g Sat); 8 mg Cholesterol; 3 g Carbohydrate; trace Fibre; trace Protein; 32 mg Sodium

Pictured on page 144.

Nibbles & Canapés

Asian Lobster Canapés

An elegant blend of lobster, ginger and chili tops rice crackers in this very sophisticated offering. Perfect for a large crowd—and a very special occasion. Assemble canapés just before serving so the rice crackers retain their pleasing crunch.

Can of frozen lobster meat, thawed, drained and squeezed dry, chopped	11.3 oz.	320 g
Can of sliced water chestnuts, drained, finely chopped	8 oz.	227 mL
Mayonnaise	1/4 cup	60 mL
Sliced green onion	2 tbsp.	30 mL
Soy sauce	1 tbsp.	15 mL
Finely grated ginger root (or 1/4 tsp., 1 mL, ground ginger)	1 tsp.	5 mL
Lime juice	1 tsp.	5 mL
Chili paste (sambal oelek)	1/2 tsp.	2 mL
Sesame rice crackers	96	96

Sliced green onion, for garnish
Roasted sesame seeds, for garnish

Combine first 8 ingredients in medium bowl.

Spoon about 1 tsp. (5 mL) lobster mixture onto each cracker.

Garnish with green onion and sesame seeds. Serve immediately. Makes 96 canapés.

1 canapé: 16 Calories; 0.5 g Total Fat (trace Mono, trace Poly, 0.1 g Sat); 3 mg Cholesterol; 2 g Carbohydrate; trace Fibre; 1 g Protein; 38 mg Sodium

Pictured at right.

1. Crab Puffs, page 44
2. Lemony Chicken Rolls, page 80
3. Asian Lobster Canapés, above
Props: Ikea

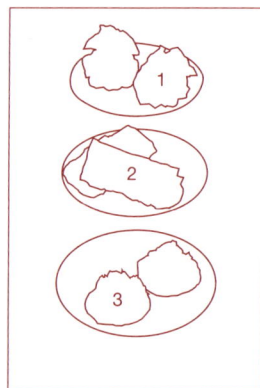

Jerk Chicken Wings

Spiced chicken wings with appetizing grill marks and lingering heat. Wings are always a crowd-pleaser—the type of appetizer that people just can't wait to dig into.

Grated onion	2 tbsp.	30 mL
Cooking oil	1 tbsp.	15 mL
Chili paste (sambal oelek)	2 tsp.	10 mL
Brown sugar, packed	1 1/2 tsp.	7 mL
Finely grated ginger root	1 tsp.	5 mL
(or 1/4 tsp., 1 mL, ground ginger)		
Dried thyme	1/2 tsp.	2 mL
Ground allspice	1/2 tsp.	2 mL
Garlic clove, minced	1	1
(or 1/4 tsp., 1 mL, powder)		
Ground cinnamon	1/4 tsp.	1 mL
Salt	1/2 tsp.	2 mL
Pepper	1/4 tsp.	1 mL
Split chicken wings, tips discarded	2 lbs.	900 g
(or chicken drumettes)		

Combine first 11 ingredients in large bowl.

Add chicken wings. Toss until coated. Preheat gas barbecue to medium-low. Arrange wings on greased grill. Close lid. Cook for about 15 minutes per side until browned and no longer pink inside. Makes about 24 wings (or 16 drumettes).

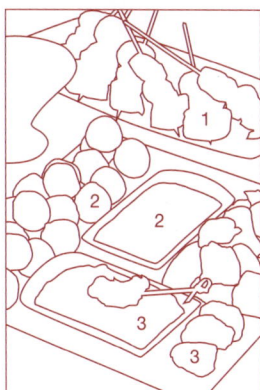

1 wing: 105 Calories; 5.9 g Total Fat (0.3 g Mono, 0.2 g Poly, 1.8 g Sat); 71 mg Cholesterol; 1 g Carbohydrate; trace Fibre; 11 g Protein; 253 mg Sodium

1. Mango Veggie Skewers, page 110
2. Falafel with Curry Yogurt, page 122
3. Bourbon Chicken Bites, page 130

Three-cheese Garlic Toasts

Crisp red pepper slivers give these intriguing little toasts a clean, attractive look. Make way for the rich and cheesy topping!

Crumbled feta cheese	1/3 cup	75 mL
Ricotta cheese	1/3 cup	75 mL
Grated Parmesan cheese	3 tbsp.	45 mL
Garlic powder	1/2 tsp.	2 mL
Whole-wheat baguette bread slices (1/4 inch, 6 mm, each)	16	16
Red pepper slivers, halved	8	8

Combine first 4 ingredients in small bowl.

Arrange bread slices on ungreased baking sheet with sides. Broil on top rack in oven for about 1 minute per side until golden. Spread cheese mixture over bread slices. Broil for about 2 minutes until edges are golden.

Garnish with red pepper. Makes 16 toasts.

1 toast: 61 Calories; 2.3 g Total Fat (0.4 g Mono, 0.2 g Poly, 1.2 g Sat); 6 mg Cholesterol; 7 g Carbohydrate; 1 g Fibre; 3 g Protein; 145 mg Sodium

Avocado Bacon Triangles

Delicious triangles with a lemony avocado spread. The intense and well-matched flavours are reminiscent of a BLT.

Whole-wheat (or white) bread slices, crusts removed	6	6
Cooking oil	2 tbsp.	30 mL
Mashed avocado	3/4 cup	175 mL
Block cream cheese, softened	1/3 cup	75 mL
Sun-dried tomatoes in oil, blotted dry, finely chopped	1/4 cup	60 mL
Dijon mustard	1 tbsp.	15 mL
Lemon juice	1 tbsp.	15 mL
Pepper	1/4 tsp.	1 mL

(continued on next page)

Finely diced seeded tomato	1/2 cup	125 mL
Bacon slices, cooked crisp and crumbled	6	6
Finely chopped chives	1 tbsp.	15 mL

Brush bread slices with cooking oil. Cut each slice diagonally into 4 triangles. Arrange on greased baking sheet with sides. Broil on top rack in oven for 1 to 2 minutes per side until golden.

Combine next 6 ingredients in small bowl. Spread over triangles.

Sprinkle with remaining 3 ingredients. Makes 24 triangles.

1 triangle: 62 Calories; 4.5 g Total Fat (2.2 g Mono, 0.7 g Poly, 1.3 g Sat); 5 mg Cholesterol; 4 g Carbohydrate; 1 g Fibre; 2 g Protein; 95 mg Sodium

Bocconcini Bruschetta

Attractive pita triangles with colourful, appetizing toppings. Along with fresh basil and tomatoes, maple syrup adds a mysterious sweetness to the mix.

Balsamic vinaigrette dressing	1/2 cup	125 mL
Maple syrup	1 tbsp.	15 mL
Dijon mustard	1 tsp.	5 mL
Garlic cloves, minced	2	2
(or 1/2 tsp., 2 mL, powder)		
Diced Roma (plum) tomato	1 cup	250 mL
Pearl bocconcini (fresh mozzarella)	1/2 cup	125 mL
Thinly sliced red onion	1/4 cup	60 mL
Chopped fresh basil	2 tbsp.	30 mL
Pita breads (7 inch, 18 cm, diameter)	2	2
Finely shredded fresh basil	3 tbsp.	45 mL

Combine first 4 ingredients in medium bowl. Add next 4 ingredients. Stir. Let stand, covered, for 30 minutes. Drain.

Place pita breads on ungreased baking sheet with sides. Bake in 400°F (200°C) oven for about 3 minutes per side until crisp. Top with tomato mixture. Cut into 6 wedges each.

Sprinkle with second amount of basil. Makes 12 wedges.

1 wedge: 59 Calories; 2.4 g Total Fat (trace Mono, 0.1 g Poly, 0.6 g Sat); 3 mg Cholesterol; 7 g Carbohydrate; trace Fibre; 2 g Protein; 86 mg Sodium

Bacon Blue Cheese Mini-quiches

These tasty quiches have the crust baked right in, making them a no-fuss option. Perfect served by themselves, or to complement an appetizer spread.

Large eggs	5	5
Biscuit mix	1/3 cup	75 mL
Milk	1/3 cup	75 mL
Salt	1/8 tsp.	0.5 mL
Pepper	1/4 tsp.	1 mL
Bacon slices, cooked crisp and crumbled	4	4
Chopped walnuts, toasted (see Tip, page 77)	1/4 cup	60 mL
Crumbled blue cheese	1/4 cup	60 mL
Finely chopped green onion	3 tbsp.	45 mL

Process first 5 ingredients in blender until smooth.

Combine remaining 4 ingredients in small bowl. Spoon into 24 well-greased mini-muffin cups. Pour egg mixture over top. Bake in 350°F (175°C) oven for about 15 minutes until knife inserted into centre of mini-quiche comes out clean. Let stand in pan on wire rack for 5 minutes. Makes 24 mini-quiches.

1 mini-quiche: 42 Calories; 2.9 g Total Fat (0.8 g Mono, 0.8 g Poly, 0.9 g Sat); 46 mg Cholesterol; 2 g Carbohydrate; trace Fibre; 2 g Protein; 95 mg Sodium

Sesame Soy Almonds

Attractive, mahogany-stained almonds with a deliciously addictive soy flavour—luckily these tasty nibbles are easy to make, because they'll vanish in no time! These will store in an airtight container at room temperature for up to three weeks.

Whole natural almonds	3 cups	750 mL
Low-sodium soy sauce	1/4 cup	60 mL
Lemon juice	1 tsp.	5 mL
Granulated sugar	1 1/2 tsp.	7 mL
Sesame oil	1 tsp.	5 mL

(continued on next page)

Nibbles & Canapés

Stir first 3 ingredients in medium bowl until coated. Transfer almonds, with slotted spoon, to greased baking sheet with sides. Reserve liquid in bowl. Bake almonds in 350°F (175°C) oven for 10 minutes, stirring once at halftime.

Add sugar and sesame oil to reserved soy sauce mixture. Stir until sugar is dissolved. Carefully add almonds. Stir until coated. Let stand for 5 minutes, stirring once. Spread almonds on same baking sheet. Bake for about 12 minutes, stirring twice, until darker brown and dry. Let stand on pan on wire rack until cool. Makes about 3 cups (750 mL).

1/2 cup (125 mL): 425 Calories; 36.7 g Total Fat (22.8 g Mono, 8.7 g Poly, 2.9 g Sat);
0 mg Cholesterol; 16 g Carbohydrate; 8 g Fibre; 16 g Protein; 356 mg Sodium

Rosemary Olives and Feta

This bold blend of mixed olives, feta and peppers could be served as-is with cocktail picks, or as part of an antipasti assortment. Many varieties of olives, such as large green and kalamata, are available in most grocery stores.

Olive oil	1/4 cup	60 mL
Lemon juice	1 tbsp.	15 mL
Finely chopped fresh rosemary	1 tsp.	5 mL
(or 1/4 tsp., 1 mL, dried, crushed)		
Grated lemon zest (see Tip, page 93)	1 tsp.	5 mL
Coarsely ground pepper	1/2 tsp.	2 mL
Garlic clove, minced	1	1
Mixed olives	2 cups	500 mL
Cubed feta cheese (1/2 inch, 12 mm, pieces)	1 cup	250 mL
Chopped roasted red peppers	1/2 cup	125 mL
(3/4 inch, 2 cm, pieces)		
Chopped fresh parsley	1/4 cup	60 mL
(or 1/2 tsp., 2 mL, flakes)		

Combine first 6 ingredients in medium bowl.

Add next 3 ingredients. Stir. Chill, covered, for 6 hours or overnight, stirring occasionally.

Add parsley. Toss. Makes about 3 1/2 cups (875 mL).

1/2 cup (125 mL): 193 Calories; 17.7 g Total Fat (11.0 g Mono, 1.3 g Poly, 5.0 g Sat);
19 mg Cholesterol; 5 g Carbohydrate; 1 g Fibre; 4 g Protein; 804 mg Sodium

Pictured on page 107.

Sweet Potato Chips with Scallops and Pea Purée

These tempting morsels will add a chic touch to your next cocktail party.

Butter	1 tbsp.	15 mL
Finely chopped onion	1/4 cup	60 mL
Garlic clove, minced	1	1
Prosciutto (or deli) ham slices, chopped	2	2
Frozen peas, thawed	1 cup	250 mL
Prepared chicken broth	3 tbsp.	45 mL
Cooking oil, for deep-frying		
Sweet potatos, peeled and thinly sliced	2	2
Salt, sprinkle		
Small sea scallops	24	24
Cooking oil	2 tbsp.	30 mL
Red pepper slices (optional)	24	24

Melt butter in large frying pan on medium-low. Add next 3 ingredients. Cook for about 3 minutes, stirring frequently, until onions are softened.

Add peas and broth. Cook for about 5 minutes until liquid is evaporated. Remove from heat. Let stand until cool enough to handle. Process in blender or food processor until almost smooth (see Safety Tip).

Pour cooking oil into deep saucepan until one-third full. Heat cooking oil on medium-high until bread cube turns brown in 1 minute (375°F, 190°C). Deep-fry sweet potato slices, in batches, for about 5 minutes until golden and crispy. Drain on paper towels. Season with salt.

Brush scallops with second amount of cooking oil. Preheat gas barbecue to medium (see Note). Cook scallops on greased grill for about 1 minute per side until lightly brown and opaque. Cut each scallop in half horizontally.

Spread 1 tbsp. (15 mL) pea mixture on each sweet potato chip. Spread 1 tsp. (5 mL) pea mixture on bottom half of each scallop. Cover with top halves of scallops. Place 1 scallop on each sweet potato chip. Garnish with red pepper. Makes 24 appetizers.

(continued on next page)

Nibbles & Canapés

1 appetizer: 60 Calories; 3 g Total Fat (1.5 g Mono; 0.5 g Poly; 0.5 g Sat); 10 mg Cholesterol; 4 g Carbohydrate; trace Fibre; 4 g Protein; 70 mg Sodium

Pictured on front cover.

Note: If you don't want to barbecue, cook the scallops with 1 tbsp. (15 mL) cooking oil in a frying pan on high for 1 minute per side until lightly brown and opaque.

Safety Tip: Follow manufacturer's instructions for processing hot liquids.

Wasabi Devilled Eggs

At last, a modern take on devilled eggs! Wasabi adds an edge to these classic flavours, and the creamy filling is topped with sophisticated garnishes.

Large hard-cooked eggs (see Tip, page 14)	12	12
Mayonnaise	1/4 cup	60 mL
Sour cream	1/4 cup	60 mL
Rice vinegar	2 tsp.	10 mL
Wasabi paste (Japanese horseradish)	1 1/2 tsp.	7 mL
Grated lemon zest	1/8 tsp.	0.5 mL
Salt	1/8 tsp.	0.5 mL

Radish, quartered and sliced, for garnish
Thinly sliced green onion, for garnish
Roasted sesame seeds, for garnish
Pickled ginger slices, for garnish (optional)

Cut eggs in half lengthwise. Transfer yolks to medium bowl. Arrange egg white halves on large plate. Mash yolks well with fork.

Add next 6 ingredients. Stir until smooth. Spoon into piping bag fitted with medium star tip (see Tip, below). Pipe into egg white halves.

Garnish with remaining 4 ingredients. Makes 24 devilled eggs.

1 devilled egg: 63 Calories; 5.1 g Total Fat (1.1 g Mono, 0.5 g Poly, 1.4 g Sat); 109 mg Cholesterol; trace Carbohydrate; 0 g Fibre; 3 g Protein; 58 mg Sodium

tip If you don't have a piping bag, you can use a freezer bag with the corner snipped off.

Crab Puffs

Lovely two-bite morsels to savour—the rich but delicate flavour of crab pairs well with dill and fresh fennel in choux *(pronounced SHOO) pastry puffs.*

CHOUX PUFFS		
Milk	1/2 cup	125 mL
Butter (or hard margarine)	2 tbsp.	30 mL
Salt	1/4 tsp.	1 mL
All-purpose flour	2/3 cup	150 mL
Dried dillweed	1/2 tsp.	2 mL
Large eggs	2	2
CRAB FENNEL FILLING		
Cooking oil	1 tsp.	5 mL
Finely chopped onion	1/2 cup	125 mL
Finely chopped fennel bulb (white part only)	1/2 cup	125 mL
Cans of crabmeat (4 1/4 oz., 120 g, each) drained, cartilage removed, flaked	2	2
Block cream cheese, softened	1/3 cup	75 mL
Grated lemon zest	1/2 tsp.	2 mL

Choux Puffs: Bring first 3 ingredients to a boil in small saucepan, stirring occasionally. Reduce heat to medium.

Add flour and dillweed. Stir vigorously for about 1 minute until mixture pulls away from side of saucepan to form soft dough. Transfer to medium bowl.

Add eggs, 1 at a time, beating well after each addition until dough is thick and glossy. Spoon into piping bag fitted with large star tip (see Tip, page 43). Pipe twenty-four 1 1/2 inch (3.8 cm) rosettes, about 1 inch (2.5 cm) apart, on parchment paper-lined baking sheet. Bake in 425°F (220°C) oven for about 10 minutes until puffed. Reduce heat to 350°F (175°C). Bake for about 10 minutes until golden and dry. Transfer to wire rack to cool. Cut small slice from top of each puff.

Crab Fennel Filling: Heat cooking oil in small frying pan on medium. Add onion and fennel. Cook for about 5 minutes, stirring often, until starting to soften. Transfer to small bowl.

(continued on next page)

Add remaining 3 ingredients. Mix well. Spoon into piping bag. Pipe into puffs. Top with puff tops. Makes 24 puffs.

1 puff: 53 Calories; 2.9 g Total Fat (0.9 g Mono, 0.2 g Poly, 1.5 g Sat); 33 mg Cholesterol; 3 g Carbohydrate; trace Fibre; 3 g Protein; 84 mg Sodium

Pictured on page 35.

Coconut Crab Cakes

Crab cakes are always a popular appetizer, but these small bites come with a tropical twist of coconut and lime!

Panko (or fine dry) bread crumbs	1/2 cup	125 mL
Mayonnaise	2 tbsp.	30 mL
Shredded coconut, toasted (see Tip, page 77)	2 tbsp.	30 mL
Sliced green onion	2 tbsp.	30 mL
Large egg, fork-beaten	1	1
Grated lime zest	1/2 tsp.	2 mL
Ground coriander	1/2 tsp.	2 mL
Salt	1/2 tsp.	2 mL
Cayenne pepper	1/8 tsp.	0.5 mL
Cans of crabmeat (4 1/4 oz., 120 g, each), drained, cartilage removed, flaked	2	2
Panko (or fine dry) bread crumbs	1/2 cup	125 mL
Cooking oil	1/4 cup	60 mL

Combine first 9 ingredients in medium bowl.

Add crab. Mix well. Divide into 16 equal portions. Shape into 1 inch (2.5 cm) diameter cakes.

Press cakes into second amount of panko crumbs in small shallow bowl until coated. Discard any remaining panko crumbs.

Heat 2 tbsp. (30 mL) cooking oil in large frying pan on medium. Cook cakes, in 2 batches, for about 2 minutes per side until golden and heated through. Transfer to large plate. Makes 16 crab cakes.

1 crab cake: 93 Calories; 6.1 g Total Fat (2.2 g Mono, 1.2 g Poly, 0.9 g Sat); 27 mg Cholesterol; 5 g Carbohydrate; trace Fibre; 4 g Protein; 186 mg Sodium

Pictured on page 53 and on back cover.

Curried Potato Bites

So delicious! These offer a great twist on traditional cracker canapés. The curry and cilantro flavours balance perfectly.

Spreadable cream cheese	1/4 cup	60 mL
Finely chopped celery	2 tbsp.	30 mL
Finely chopped red onion	2 tbsp.	30 mL
Finely chopped yellow pepper	2 tbsp.	30 mL
Mayonnaise	2 tbsp.	30 mL
Lime juice	2 tsp.	10 mL
Mild curry paste	2 tsp.	10 mL
Granulated sugar	1/2 tsp.	2 mL
Ground cumin	1/8 tsp.	0.5 mL
Pepper	1/8 tsp.	0.5 mL
Red baby potatoes, halved	1 lb.	454 g
Salt	1 tsp.	5 mL

Cilantro (or parsley) leaves, for garnish

Combine first 10 ingredients in small bowl. Chill.

Pour water into large saucepan until about 1 inch (2.5 cm) deep. Add potatoes and salt. Bring to a boil. Reduce heat to medium. Boil gently, covered, for 12 to 15 minutes until tender. Drain. Rinse with cold water. Drain well. Trim bottom of each potato half to make flat. Arrange potatoes, trimmed-side down, on serving platter. Spoon about 1 tsp. (5 mL) cream cheese mixture onto each potato half.

Garnish with cilantro leaves. Makes about 34 bites.

1 bite: 24 Calories; 1.3 g Total Fat (0.2 g Mono, trace Poly, 0.5 g Sat); 2 mg Cholesterol; 3 g Carbohydrate; trace Fibre; trace Protein; 20 mg Sodium

Mushroom Leek Crostini

Indulge in this delicious combination—mushroom and leek with a lemony flavour and peppery finish are scrumptious atop toasted baguette slices.

Cooking oil	2 tsp.	10 mL
Thinly sliced leek (white part only)	1 cup	250 mL
Garlic clove, minced	1	1
(or 1/4 tsp., 1 mL, powder)		
Chopped portobello mushrooms	2 1/2 cups	625 mL
Sliced fresh white mushrooms	2 1/2 cups	625 mL
Chopped fresh parsley	2 tbsp.	30 mL
(or 1 1/2 tsp., 7 mL, flakes)		
Sour cream	2 tbsp.	30 mL
Lemon juice	2 tsp.	10 mL
Salt	1/8 tsp.	0.5 mL
Pepper	1/4 tsp.	1 mL
Baguette bread slices, cut diagonally,	24	24
1/4 inch (6 mm) each		

Heat cooking oil in large frying pan on medium. Add leek. Cook for about 5 minutes, stirring often, until softened.

Add garlic. Heat and stir for 1 minute. Add portobello and white mushrooms. Cook for about 12 minutes, stirring occasionally, until liquid is evaporated.

Add next 5 ingredients. Stir. Remove from heat.

Arrange bread slices on ungreased baking sheet. Broil on top rack in oven for about 1 minute per side until golden. Spoon mushroom mixture over top. Makes 24 crostini.

1 crostini: 40 Calories; 1.0 g Total Fat (0.2 g Mono, 0.1 g Poly, 0.2 g Sat); 2 mg Cholesterol; 7 g Carbohydrate; trace Fibre; 1 g Protein; 72 mg Sodium

Pesto Mascarpone Bites

Nothing compares to mascarpone's decadent texture and flavour. Indulge in these pumpernickel slices topped with a cheesy blend and fresh basil.

Cooking oil	1/4 tsp.	1 mL
Chopped prosciutto (or deli) ham	1/2 cup	125 mL
Mascarpone cheese	1/2 cup	125 mL
Milk	2 tbsp.	30 mL
Basil pesto	2 tsp.	10 mL
Pumpernickel cocktail bread slices (see Note)	12	12
Fresh basil leaves, for garnish	12	12

Heat cooking oil in small frying pan on medium. Add prosciutto. Cook, stirring occasionally, until crisp. Transfer to paper towel-lined plate to drain.

Combine next 3 ingredients and prosciutto in small bowl. Spread over bread slices.

Garnish with basil. Makes 12 bites.

1 bite: 114 Calories; 9.6 g Total Fat (0.1 g Mono, 0.1 g Poly, 4.9 g Sat); 28 mg Cholesterol; 4 g Carbohydrate; trace Fibre; 4 g Protein; 134 mg Sodium

Pictured on page 54.

Note: If you can't find cocktail pumpernickel, cut pumpernickel bread slices into twelve 2 inch (5 cm) squares.

Peppery Pita Chips

Crisp, lightly seasoned pita chips are a healthy dipper that would pair wonderfully with Beautiful Beet Dip, page 15, or Shrimp Ceviche, page 97.

Dried basil	1/4 tsp.	1 mL
Pepper	1/4 tsp.	1 mL
Garlic powder	1/8 tsp.	0.5 mL
Onion salt	1/8 tsp.	0.5 mL
Pita breads (7 inch, 18 cm, diameter)	4	4
Cooking spray		

(continued on next page)

Combine first 4 ingredients in small cup.

Spray 1 side of each pita with cooking spray. Sprinkle with basil mixture. Cut each pita into 8 wedges. Arrange in single layer on greased baking sheet. Bake in 375°F (190°C) oven for about 10 minutes until crisp and golden. Makes 32 chips.

1 chip: 21 Calories; 0.1 g Total Fat (trace Mono, trace Poly, trace Sat); 0 mg Cholesterol; 4 g Carbohydrate; trace Fibre; 1 g Protein; 43 mg Sodium

Salmon Pesto Pastries

Dill adds a delicate touch of colour to this gorgeous salmon-topped pastry.

Chopped fresh dill, lightly packed	1/3 cup	75 mL
Pine nuts, toasted (see Tip, page 77)	1/4 cup	60 mL
Olive (or cooking) oil	2 tbsp.	30 mL
Lemon juice	2 tsp.	10 mL
Dijon mustard	1 tsp.	5 mL
Garlic clove, minced	1	1
(or 1/4 tsp., 1 mL, powder)		
Grated Parmesan cheese	1/4 cup	60 mL
Package of puff pastry (14 oz., 397 g), thawed according to package directions	1/2	1/2
Salmon fillets, skin and any small bones removed, cut into 12 pieces	1/2 lb.	225 g
Sprigs of fresh dill, for garnish	12	12

Process first 6 ingredients in food processor until smooth. Transfer to small bowl. Add cheese. Stir.

Roll out pastry on lightly floured surface to 8 x 10 inch (20 x 25 cm) rectangle. Cut into 12 squares. Arrange, about 1 inch (2.5 cm) apart, on greased baking sheet with sides. Spread dill mixture over squares. Place fish pieces in centre of dill mixture. Bake in 400°F (200°C) oven for about 15 minutes until pastry is puffed and golden and fish flakes easily when tested with fork.

Garnish with dill sprigs. Makes 12 pastries.

1 pastry: 144 Calories; 10.7 g Total Fat (2.7 g Mono, 1.7 g Poly, 2.2 g Sat); 12 mg Cholesterol; 6 g Carbohydrate; trace Fibre; 7 g Protein; 137 mg Sodium

Pictured on page 54.

Stuffed Shrimp

These appetizing shrimp are stuffed with plenty of herb and garlic flavour.
A sophisticated cocktail party offering.

Block cream cheese, softened	2 tbsp.	30 mL
Crumbled feta cheese	2 tbsp.	30 mL
Fine dry bread crumbs	1 tbsp.	15 mL
Chopped fresh basil	2 tsp.	10 mL
(or 1/2 tsp., 2 mL, dried)		
Chopped fresh parsley	1 tsp.	5 mL
(or 1/4 tsp., 1 mL, dried)		
Grated lemon zest	1/4 tsp.	1 mL
Garlic powder	1/8 tsp.	0.5 mL
Pepper	1/8 tsp.	0.5 mL
Uncooked extra-large shrimp	12	12
(peeled and deveined), tails intact		
Cooking spray		

Combine first 8 ingredients in small bowl.

Cut along backs of shrimp, almost, but not quite through to other side. Press cheese mixture along cut sides of shrimp. Arrange on greased baking sheet with sides. Spray with cooking spray. Broil on centre rack in oven for about 4 minutes until shrimp turn pink and cheese mixture starts to brown. Makes 12 shrimp.

1 shrimp: 23 Calories; 1.4 g Total Fat (0.3 g Mono, 0.1 g Poly, 0.8 g Sat); 15 mg Cholesterol; 1 g Carbohydrate; trace Fibre; 2 g Protein; 39 mg Sodium

Pictured on page 53 and on back cover.

Sweet and Smoky Nut Mix

Simple ingredients with lots of punch! This blend of roasted nuts has a surprising hint of sweet orange that enhances the smoky flavours.

Large egg white	1	1
Raw cashews	2 cups	500 mL
Pecan halves	1 cup	250 mL
Whole natural almonds	1 cup	250 mL

(continued on next page)

Sweetened orange drink crystals	1/4 cup	60 mL
Smoked (sweet) paprika	1 1/2 tsp.	7 mL
Salt	1/2 tsp.	2 mL
Cayenne pepper	1/8 tsp.	0.5 mL

Beat egg white in large bowl until frothy. Add next 3 ingredients. Stir.

Add remaining 4 ingredients. Stir until coated. Spread evenly on greased baking sheet with sides. Bake in 350°F (175°C) oven for about 15 minutes, stirring occasionally, until golden. Makes about 4 cups (1 L).

1/4 cup (60 mL): 229 Calories; 18.7 g Total Fat (10.7 g Mono, 4.2 g Poly, 2.4 g Sat); 0 mg Cholesterol; 12 g Carbohydrate; 2 g Fibre; 7 g Protein; 79 mg Sodium

Pictured on page 107.

Creamy Goat Cheese Bowls

These cute, colourful appies have the delicious contrast of creamy goat cheese and fresh tomatoes. Prepared bruschetta topping could be used in place of the tomato and balsamic vinegar.

Bag of bowl-shaped tortilla chips (9 oz., 255 g)	1/2	1/2
Block cream cheese, softened	4 oz.	125 g
Goat (chèvre) cheese, softened	4 oz.	113 g
Dried basil	1/2 tsp.	2 mL
Dried oregano	1/2 tsp.	2 mL
Chopped tomato, seeds removed	1 cup	250 mL
Balsamic vinegar	1 tsp.	5 mL
Chopped fresh parsley, for garnish		

Arrange tortilla chips in single layer on ungreased baking sheet with sides.

Combine next 4 ingredients in small bowl. Spoon into tortilla chips. Bake in 350°F (175°C) oven for about 15 minutes until cheese mixture is golden on edges.

Toss tomato and vinegar in separate small bowl. Scatter over cheese mixture.

Sprinkle with parsley. Makes about 40 goat cheese bowls.

1 goat cheese bowl: 37 Calories; 2.6 g Total Fat (0.8 g Mono, 0.4 g Poly, 1.3 g Sat); 5 mg Cholesterol; 2 g Carbohydrate; trace Fibre; 1 g Protein; 37 mg Sodium

Spicy Mini Tuna Cakes

Peppers and chilies provide colour and gentle heat to these tasty mini-cakes with a crisp coating. Serve with a cool sour cream-based dip.

Large egg, fork-beaten	1	1
Fine dry bread crumbs	1/2 cup	125 mL
Finely chopped red pepper	1/4 cup	60 mL
Finely chopped yellow pepper	1/4 cup	60 mL
Mayonnaise	2 tbsp.	30 mL
Finely chopped green onion	1 tbsp.	15 mL
Dried crushed chilies	1/4 tsp.	1 mL
Paprika	1/4 tsp.	1 mL
Cans of flaked light tuna in water (6 oz., 170 g, each), drained	2	2
Fine dry bread crumbs	1/3 cup	75 mL
Cooking oil	1/4 cup	60 mL

Combine first 8 ingredients in medium bowl.

Add tuna. Mix well. Roll into balls, using about 1 tbsp. (15 mL) for each. Shape into 1 1/2 inch (3.8 cm) diameter cakes. Chill for 30 minutes.

Put bread crumbs into small shallow bowl. Press cakes in bread crumbs until coated.

Heat cooking oil in medium frying pan on medium. Cook cakes, in 2 batches, for about 3 minutes per side until browned. Makes about 28 tuna cakes.

1 tuna cake: 56 Calories; 3.5 g Total Fat (1.3 g Mono, 0.8 g Poly, 0.4 g Sat); 13 mg Cholesterol; 2 g Carbohydrate; trace Fibre; 4 g Protein; 76 mg Sodium

1. Stuffed Shrimp, page 50
2. Grape Pistachio Bites, page 32
3. Coconut Crab Cakes, page 45

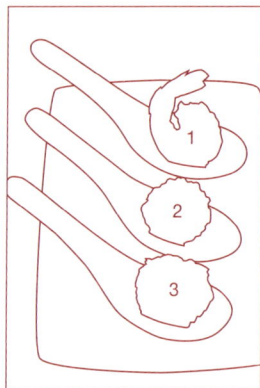

Triple Chili Squares

Here's a square that you'd never find on a dessert tray! These savoury nibbles are moist and quiche-like with egg, cheese and chili spice.

Large eggs	4	4
Ricotta cheese	1 cup	250 mL
All-purpose flour	1/2 cup	125 mL
Sliced green onion	1/2 cup	125 mL
Cooking oil	2 tbsp.	30 mL
Chili powder	1 tbsp.	15 mL
Baking powder	1/2 tsp.	2 mL
Dried crushed chilies	1/2 tsp.	2 mL
Baking soda	1/4 tsp.	1 mL
Salt	1/4 tsp.	1 mL
Pepper	1/4 tsp.	1 mL
Grated jalapeño Monterey Jack cheese	1 1/2 cups	375 mL
Can of diced green chilies	4 oz.	113 g

Whisk first 11 ingredients in medium bowl until combined.

Add Monterey Jack cheese and green chilies. Stir until combined. Spread evenly in greased 9 x 9 inch (23 x 23 cm) pan. Bake in 350°F (175°C) oven for about 45 minutes until wooden pick inserted in centre comes out clean. Let stand in pan on wire rack for about 15 minutes until slightly cooled. Cuts into 25 squares.

1 square: 71 Calories; 5.2 g Total Fat (1.0 g Mono, 0.5 g Poly, 2.3 g Sat); 44 mg Cholesterol; 2 g Carbohydrate; trace Fibre; 4 g Protein; 138 mg Sodium

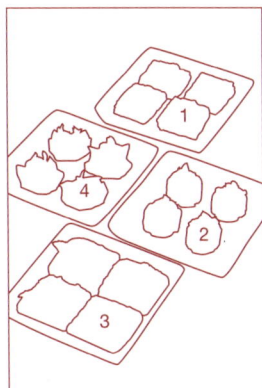

1. Salmon Pesto Pastries, page 49
2. Salmon Cucumber Cups, page 32
3. Pesto Mascarpone Bites, page 48
4. Steamed Chicken Dumplings, page 57

Props: Ikea

Italian Herbed Flatbread

Sometimes a simple seasoned bread is just the thing to nibble on at a casual gathering. This crisp, light-textured flatbread is delicious with Italian seasonings, garlic and Parmesan.

All-purpose flour	1 3/4 cup	425 mL
Envelope of instant yeast (or 2 1/4 tsp., 11 mL)	1/4 oz.	8 g
Italian seasoning	1 tsp.	5 mL
Granulated sugar	1/2 tsp.	2 mL
Lemon pepper	1/4 tsp.	1 mL
Very warm water (see Note)	2/3 cup	150 mL
Olive (or cooking) oil	2 tsp.	10 mL
Olive (or cooking) oil	1 tbsp.	15 mL
Olive (or cooking) oil	1 tbsp.	15 mL
Grated Parmesan cheese	2 tbsp.	30 mL
Coarse salt	1 tsp.	5 mL
Italian seasoning	1 tsp.	5 mL

Combine first 5 ingredients in large bowl.

Combine water and first amount of olive oil in small cup. Add to flour mixture. Stir until soft dough forms. Turn out onto lightly floured surface. Knead for 8 to 10 minutes until smooth and elastic. Cover with greased waxed paper and tea towel. Let stand for 10 minutes. Roll out dough to 12 inch (30 cm) circle. Place on greased pizza pan.

Brush with second amount of olive oil. Cover with greased waxed paper and tea towel. Let stand in oven with light on and door closed for 20 minutes. Poke indentations in surface of dough with fingers.

Brush with third amount of olive oil. Sprinkle with remaining 3 ingredients. Bake in 425°F (220°C) oven for about 15 minutes until golden. Cuts into 16 wedges.

1 wedge: 70 Calories; 2.6 g Total Fat (1.8 g Mono, 0.2 g Poly, 0.5 g Sat); 1 mg Cholesterol; 10 g Carbohydrate; trace Fibre; 2 g Protein; 167 mg Sodium

Note: When using yeast, it is important for the liquid to be at the correct temperature. If the liquid is too cool, the yeast will not activate properly. If the liquid is too hot, the yeast will be destroyed. For best results, follow the recommended temperatures as instructed on the package.

Nibbles & Canapés

Steamed Chicken Dumplings

These cute dumplings are packed with the pleasing Asian flavours of ginger, garlic and soy. Perfect dim sum fare with an appealing look.

Finely chopped water chestnuts	2 tbsp.	30 mL
Soy sauce	4 tsp.	20 mL
Finely chopped green onion	1 tbsp.	15 mL
Rice wine vinegar	2 tsp.	10 mL
Cornstarch	1 tsp.	5 mL
Finely grated ginger root	1/2 tsp.	2 mL
(or 1/8 tsp., 0.5 mL, ground ginger)		
Garlic clove, minced	1	1
(or 1/4 tsp., 1 mL, powder)		
Lean ground chicken	1/2 lb.	225 g
Round dumpling wrappers	12	12

Combine first 7 ingredients in medium bowl.

Add chicken. Mix well.

Arrange wrappers on work surface. Place about 1 tbsp. (15 mL) chicken mixture in centre of each wrapper. Dampen edges with water. Gather up wrappers around filling, pinching to make small pleats, leaving top slightly open. Tap dumplings gently on work surface to flatten bottom slightly. Arrange dumplings, evenly spaced apart, in greased 9 x 9 inch (23 x 23 cm) pan, being careful dumplings do not touch sides of pan. Place wire rack in bottom of roasting pan. Pour water into roasting pan until about 1 inch (2.5 cm) deep. Bring to a boil on stovetop. Set baking pan on wire rack. Cook, covered, on medium for about 8 minutes until filling is no longer pink and internal temperature reaches 175°F (80°C). Makes 12 dumplings.

1 dumpling: 50 Calories; 1.5 g Total Fat (0 g Mono, 0 g Poly, 0.4 g Sat); 13 mg Cholesterol; 5 g Carbohydrate; trace Fibre; 4 g Protein; 197 mg Sodium

Pictured on page 54.

Lemon Pepper Roulade

If you want to present something truly unique at your party, look no further than these savoury spirals with lemon freshness and a creamy filling.

Egg whites (large), room temperature	2	2
Egg yolks (large)	2	2
Milk	1/4 cup	60 mL
All-purpose flour	3 tbsp.	45 mL
Granulated sugar	1 tsp.	5 mL
Grated lemon zest (see Tip, page 93)	1/2 tsp.	2 mL
Salt	1/8 tsp.	0.5 mL
Spreadable cream cheese	2 tbsp.	30 mL
Chopped fresh chives (or green onion)	1 tsp.	5 mL
Lemon juice	1/2 tsp.	2 mL
Coarsely ground pepper	1/4 tsp.	1 mL
Grated lemon zest (see Tip, page 93)	1/8 tsp.	0.5 mL

Beat egg whites in small bowl until stiff peaks form.

Using same beaters, beat egg yolks in separate small bowl until thick and pale. Add next 5 ingredients. Beat on low until smooth. Fold into egg whites until no white streaks remain. Spread evenly in greased 9 x 13 inch (23 x 33 cm) pan. Bake in 375°F (190°C) oven for about 7 minutes until edges start to pull away from sides of pan. Let stand for 5 minutes. Remove from pan.

Stir remaining 5 ingredients in small cup until smooth. Spread over egg mixture. Roll up tightly, jelly-roll style, from short side. Cuts into twelve 1/2 inch (12 mm) slices.

1 slice: 182 Calories; 9.8 g Total Fat (2.1 g Mono, 0.7 g Poly, 5.3 g Sat); 222 mg Cholesterol; 14 g Carbohydrate; trace Fibre; 10 g Protein; 275 mg Sodium

Rolls, Wraps & Stacks

Phyllo Pizza Strips

Pizza need not be heavy—these light, crisp strips need only a sprinkle of intensely flavoured roasted tomatoes, Asiago and fresh arugula.

Olive (or cooking) oil	1 1/2 tsp.	7 mL
Garlic powder	1/8 tsp.	0.5 mL
Pepper	1/8 tsp.	0.5 mL
Grape tomatoes, halved	20	20
Pearl onions, quartered	20	20
Phyllo pastry sheets, thawed according to package directions	8	8
Butter (or hard margarine), melted	1/3 cup	75 mL
Grated Asiago cheese	1/2 cup	125 mL
Grated Asiago cheese	1 cup	250 mL
Chopped arugula, lightly packed	1/2 cup	125 mL

Combine first 3 ingredients in medium bowl.

Add tomato and onion. Toss until coated. Transfer to ungreased baking sheet with sides. Cook in 450°F (230°C) oven for about 10 minutes until onion is softened and browned. Set aside.

Place 1 pastry sheet on separate greased baking sheet with sides. Cover remaining sheets with damp towel to prevent drying. Brush sheet with butter. Sprinkle with 1 tbsp. (15 mL) cheese. Place second pastry sheet over top. Brush with butter. Sprinkle with 1 tbsp. (15 mL) cheese. Repeat with remaining pastry sheets, butter and first amount of cheese. Scatter tomato mixture over cheese, leaving 1 inch (2.5 cm) edge on all sides.

Sprinkle with second amount of cheese. Bake in 400°F (200°C) oven for about 15 minutes until pastry is golden and edges are crisp.

Sprinkle arugula over top. Let stand on baking sheet for 5 minutes before transfering to cutting board. Cut lengthwise into 3 rectangles. Cut rectangles crosswise into 2 inch (5 cm) strips. Makes about 24 pizza strips.

1 pizza strip: 79 Calories; 5.5 g Total Fat (1.1 g Mono, 0.2 g Poly, 3.0 g Sat); 13 mg Cholesterol; 5 g Carbohydrate; trace Fibre; 2 g Protein; 118 mg Sodium

Beef Empanada Tarts

This big batch of beef and olive tarts is a fantastic make-ahead option—just cool the baked tarts and freeze them without the olive garnish.

Cooking oil	2 tsp.	10 mL
Lean ground beef	1 lb.	454 g
Chopped onion	1 cup	250 mL
Prepared beef broth	1 cup	250 mL
Chopped sliced green olives	1/3 cup	75 mL
Chopped dark raisins	1/4 cup	60 mL
Tomato paste (see Tip, page 111)	2 tbsp.	30 mL
Red wine vinegar	1 tbsp.	15 mL
Chopped fresh oregano	1 tbsp.	15 mL
(or 3/4 tsp., 4 mL, dried)		
Paprika	1 tsp.	5 mL
Ground cumin	1/2 tsp.	2 mL
Salt	1/2 tsp.	2 mL
Pepper	1/2 tsp.	2 mL
Garlic clove, minced	1	1
(or 1/4 tsp., 1 mL, powder)		
Large hard-cooked eggs (see Tip, page 14), chopped	2	2
Frozen mini tart shells	40	40
Sliced green olives (optional)	1/4 cup	60 mL

Heat cooking oil in large saucepan on medium. Add beef and onion. Scramble-fry for about 8 minutes until beef is no longer pink.

Add next 11 ingredients. Stir. Cook, partially covered, for about 10 minutes, stirring occasionally, until liquid is almost evaporated. Remove from heat.

Add eggs. Stir.

Arrange tart shells on ungreased baking sheets with sides. Bake in 400°F (200°C) oven for about 12 minutes until golden. Fill tart shells with beef mixture. Bake for about 5 minutes until heated through (see Note).

Garnish with second amount of olive slices. Makes 40 tarts.

(continued on next page)

Rolls, Wraps & Stacks

1 tart: 42 Calories; 2.6 g Total Fat (0.4 g Mono, 0.1 g Poly, 0.9 g Sat); 18 mg Cholesterol;
2 g Carbohydrate; trace Fibre; 3 g Protein; 94 mg Sodium

Note: Reheat from frozen in 375°F (190°C) oven for about 15 minutes until golden and heated through. Garnish with olive slices. Alternately, use only half the filling for 20 tarts, and freeze leftover filling in an airtight container for up to 3 months.

Steak Sandwich Minis

These small, open-faced sandwiches are as delicious as they look! Tender beef pairs with tangy horseradish sauce to create a filling appetizer with great savoury flavours.

Cooking oil	1 tbsp.	15 mL
Beef strip loin steak, trimmed of fat	1 lb.	454 g
Montreal steak spice, sprinkle		
Thinly sliced red onion	1/2 cup	125 mL
Sour cream	1/4 cup	60 mL
Mayonnaise	2 tbsp.	30 mL
Finely chopped green onion	1 tbsp.	15 mL
Prepared horseradish	1 tbsp.	15 mL
Dijon mustard	2 tsp.	10 mL
Baguette bread slices, cut diagonally (3/4 inch, 2 cm, each)	20	20

Heat cooking oil in large frying pan on medium-high. Sprinkle both sides of steak with steak spice. Add to frying pan. Cook for 4 to 5 minutes per side until internal temperature reaches 160°F (71°C) for medium or until steak reaches desired doneness. Transfer to cutting board. Cover with foil. Let stand for 10 minutes. Cut in half lengthwise. Slice thinly across the grain.

Add onion to same frying pan on medium. Cook for about 3 minutes, stirring often, until golden. Transfer to paper towel-lined plate to drain.

Combine next 5 ingredients in small bowl.

Arrange bread slices on serving platter. Top with beef, sour cream mixture and onion. Makes 20 mini-sandwiches.

1 mini-sandwich: 86 Calories; 3.6 g Total Fat (0.7 g Mono, 0.2 g Poly, 0.9 g Sat); 11 mg Cholesterol;
7 g Carbohydrate; trace Fibre; 6 g Protein; 96 mg Sodium

Jerk Chicken Sandwiches

Fresh, attractive croissant sandwiches are filled with crisp green lettuce and sweetly spiced jerk chicken—these would make a pretty addition to a luncheon. Use different small rolls if mini-croissants are unavailable.

Brown sugar, packed	1 tbsp.	15 mL
Dried thyme	1 tsp.	5 mL
Ground allspice	1 tsp.	5 mL
Ground ginger	1 tsp.	5 mL
Garlic powder	3/4 tsp.	4 mL
Dried crushed chilies	1/2 tsp.	2 mL
Ground cinnamon	1/2 tsp.	2 mL
Salt	1/2 tsp.	2 mL
Pepper	1/4 tsp.	1 mL
Cooking oil	1 tbsp.	15 mL
Boneless, skinless chicken breast halves (4 – 6 oz., 113 – 170 g, each)	2	2
Mayonnaise	1/2 cup	125 mL
Lime juice	1 tbsp.	15 mL
Mini-croissants, split	12	12
Green leaf lettuce leaves, quartered	3	3
Thinly sliced yellow pepper	1/2 cup	125 mL

Combine first 9 ingredients in small bowl.

Transfer half of brown sugar mixture to large bowl. Add cooking oil to same large bowl. Stir. Add chicken. Toss until coated. Marinate, covered, in refrigerator for 1 hour. Remove chicken. Arrange on greased baking sheet with sides. Discard any remaining marinade. Cook in 425°F (220°C) oven for about 15 minutes until internal temperature reaches 170°F (77°C). Let stand for 5 minutes. Cut crosswise into thin slices.

Add mayonnaise and lime juice to remaining sugar mixture. Stir. Spread over cut sides of croissants. Layer lettuce, yellow pepper and chicken on bottom halves of croissants. Cover with tops. Secure with wooden picks. Makes 12 sandwiches.

1 sandwich: 223 Calories; 14.8 g Total Fat (2.3 g Mono, 0.7 g Poly, 4.5 g Sat); 33 mg Cholesterol; 15 g Carbohydrate; 1 g Fibre; 7 g Protein; 372 mg Sodium

Pictured on page 71.

Zippy Mustard Spirals

Baked and served hot, these attractive little spirals are crunchy on the outside with a delicious, savoury flavour. When served cold, without baking, the pickled asparagus flavour really comes through. Try them both ways!

Cooking oil	1 tsp.	5 mL
Lean ground beef	1/2 lb.	225 g
Pepper	1/4 tsp.	1 mL
Block cream cheese, softened	4 oz.	125 g
Dijon mustard	2 tbsp.	30 mL
Prepared horseradish	1 tbsp.	15 mL
Flour tortillas (9 inch, 23 cm, diameter)	4	4
Grated smoked Gouda cheese	1 cup	250 mL
Pickled asparagus spears	12	12
Cooking oil	2 tsp.	10 mL

Heat first amount of cooking oil in medium frying pan on medium. Add beef and pepper. Scramble-fry for about 10 minutes until beef is no longer pink. Drain. Transfer to small bowl. Cool.

Combine next 3 ingredients in small bowl. Spread over tortillas.

Add Gouda cheese to beef mixture. Stir. Scatter over cream cheese mixture.

Place 3 asparagus spears horizontally near bottom edge of each tortilla. Roll up tightly, jelly roll-style, to enclose filling. Press seams against rolls to seal. Wrap each roll with plastic wrap. Chill for about 2 hours until firm. Discard plastic wrap. Trim ends of each roll. Cut each roll into ten 1/2 inch (12 mm) slices. Arrange, cut-side up, on greased baking sheet.

Brush with second amount of cooking oil. Bake in 350°F (175°C) oven for about 15 minutes until edges are golden. Makes 40 spirals.

1 spiral: 51 Calories; 3.3 g Total Fat (1.1 g Mono, 0.4 g Poly, 1.6 g Sat); 10 mg Cholesterol; 3 g Carbohydrates; trace Fibre; 3 g Protein, 90 mg Sodium

Spicy BLT Stacks

Everyone loves the classic flavours of a BLT—and there's no doubt these mini-sandwiches will stack up to all expectations! This version is a little spiced up with the addition of chilies and a creamy Dijon bite.

Bacon slices, cooked crisp and crumbled	4	4
Mayonnaise	3 tbsp.	45 mL
Dijon mustard	1 tbsp.	15 mL
Dried crushed chilies	1/2 tsp.	2 mL
Liquid honey	1/2 tsp.	2 mL
Whole-wheat bread slices, crusts removed, toasted	4	4
Cherry tomato slices	12	12
Butter lettuce leaves	2	2

Combine first 5 ingredients in small bowl. Spread over toast slices.

Layer tomato slices and lettuce leaves over mayonnaise mixture on 2 toast slices. Cover with remaining toast slices. Cut each sandwich into 6 pieces. Secure with wooden picks. Makes 12 stacks.

1 stack: 62 Calories; 4.1 g Total Fat (0.6 g Mono, 0.2 g Poly, 0.8 g Sat); 4 mg Cholesterol; 5 g Carbohydrate; 1 g Fibre; 2 g Protein; 133 mg Sodium

Mini Reuben Stacks

A few simple ingredients combine to create little stacks packed with the classic flavours of a Reuben sandwich.

Pumpernickel cocktail bread slices (see Note)	16	16
Dijon mustard	2 tbsp.	30 mL
Mayonnaise	2 tbsp.	30 mL
Thinly sliced deli corned beef	4 oz.	113 g
Sauerkraut, drained	1/3 cup	75 mL
Deli Swiss cheese slices, quartered (about 3 1/4 oz., 92 g)	4	4

(continued on next page)

Arrange bread slices in single layer on ungreased baking sheet with sides. Broil on top rack in oven for about 1 minute per side until crisp.

Combine mustard and mayonnaise in small bowl. Spread over bread slices.

Layer remaining 3 ingredients, in order given, over mustard mixture. Broil for about 2 minutes until cheese is melted. Makes 16 stacks.

1 stack: 61 Calories; 3.4 g Total Fat (0.1 g Mono, 0.1 g Poly, 1.4 g Sat); 9 mg Cholesterol; 4 g Carbohydrate; 1 g Fibre; 3 g Protein; 184 mg Sodium

Note: If you can't find cocktail pumpernickel, cut pumpernickel bread slices into sixteen 2 inch (5 cm) squares.

Greek Sausage Parcels

Transform a few everyday ingredients into extraordinary little appetizers! These tasty sausage and pastry triangles are loaded with lovely Greek flavours.

Frozen unsweetened tart shells (3 inch, 7.5 cm, diameter)	**16**	**16**
Chorizo (or hot Italian) sausage, casing removed	**1/2 lb.**	**225 g**
Frozen chopped spinach, thawed and squeezed dry	**1/2 cup**	**125 mL**
Crumbled feta cheese	**1/4 cup**	**60 mL**
Grated lemon zest	**2 tsp.**	**10 mL**
Red pepper slivers	**16**	**16**

Remove frozen tart shells from foil cups. Let stand, covered, for 10 to 15 minutes until pliable.

Combine next 4 ingredients in small bowl. Spoon sausage mixture into centre of each tart shell. Fold edges toward centre in 3 sections, forming a triangle. Pinch edges firmly to seal, leaving opening in centre.

Press red pepper over filling. Arrange on ungreased baking sheet with sides. Bake in 400°F (200°C) oven for about 20 minutes until pastry is golden and filling is no longer pink inside. Makes 16 parcels.

1 parcel: 139 Calories; 9.5 g Total Fat (0.1 g Mono, trace Poly, 2.9 g Sat); 10 mg Cholesterol; 10 g Carbohydrate; trace Fibre; 1 g Protein; 278 mg Sodium

Grape Leaf Cigars

These compact grape leaf rolls are packed with a deliciously lemony blend of beef and rice—savoury bites that are great on their own or served with tzatziki for dipping.

Long-grain white rice	1/2 cup	125 mL
Boiling water	1 cup	250 mL
Dried mint leaves	2 tsp.	10 mL
Garlic clove, minced	1	1
(or 1/4 tsp., 1 mL, powder)		
Ground cinnamon	1/4 tsp.	1 mL
Salt	3/4 tsp.	4 mL
Pepper	1/8 tsp	0.5 mL
Lean ground beef	1/2 lb.	225 g
Grape leaves, rinsed and drained, tough stems removed	42	42
Boiling water	1 cup	250 mL
Lemon juice	1/4 cup	60 mL

Put rice into small heatproof bowl. Add first amount of boiling water. Stir. Let stand for 15 minutes. Drain. Rinse with cold water. Drain well.

Combine next 5 ingredients in medium bowl.

Add beef and rice. Mix well. Divide into 1 1/2 tsp. (7 mL) portions. Shape into 3 inch (7.5 cm) long logs.

Place 1 leaf on work surface, vein-side up, stem-side closest to you. Place 1 log across leaf, about 1/2 inch (12 mm) from bottom. Fold bottom of leaf over beef mixture. Fold in sides. Roll up tightly from bottom to enclose filling. Place, seam-side down, in shallow 2 quart (2 L) baking dish. Repeat with remaining leaves and filling.

Pour second amount of boiling water over top. Cook, covered, in 325°F (160°C) oven for 25 minutes.

Drizzle with lemon juice. Cook, covered, for about 30 minutes until rice is tender and beef is no longer pink. Let stand, covered, for 10 minutes. Makes about 42 stuffed grape leaves.

1 stuffed grape leaf: 22 Calories; 0.9 g Total Fat (0 g Mono, trace Poly, 0.3 g Sat); 4 mg Cholesterol; 2 g Carbohydrate; trace Fibre; 1 g Protein; 45 mg Sodium

Rolls, Wraps & Stacks

Shrimp Onion Triangles

Tasty, gingery triangles with delicious Asian flavours and tender shrimp. There will be two wrapper squares left over that you can either discard or save for another use.

Uncooked shrimp (peeled and deveined)	1/2 lb.	225 g
Chopped green onion	1 tbsp.	15 mL
Finely grated ginger root	2 tsp.	10 mL
(or 1/2 tsp., 2 mL, ground ginger)		
Sesame oil (for flavour)	1/2 tsp.	2 mL
Salt, sprinkle		
Pepper	1/8 tsp.	0.5 mL
Spring roll wrappers (6 inch,	5	5
15 cm, square), quartered		

Cooking spray

Place first 6 ingredients in food processor. Process with on/off motion until finely chopped.

Place 1 wrapper on work surface. Cover remaining wrappers with damp towel to prevent drying. Spread about 2 tsp. (10 mL) shrimp mixture over 1 corner of wrapper, leaving 1/2 inch (12 mm) edge (see diagram). Dampen edges with water. Fold opposite corner over filling to form triangle. Press edges to seal. Repeat with remaining wrappers and shrimp mixture. Arrange on greased baking sheets with sides.

Spray with cooking spray. Bake in 425°F (220°C) oven for about 10 minutes until edges are golden and filling is pink. Makes 18 triangles.

1 triangle: 37 Calories; 0.5 g Total Fat (0.1 g Mono, 0.1 g Poly, 0.1 g Sat); 20 mg Cholesterol; 5 g Carbohydrate; trace Fibre; 3 g Protein; 61 mg Sodium

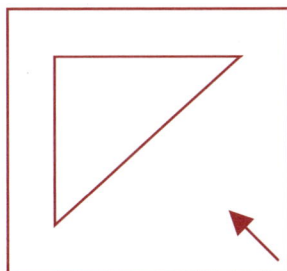

Cajun Sausage Rolls

These two-bite sausage rolls are made with beef and can be served hot or chilled. A sprinkling of spice on the outside hints at the Cajun flavours tucked inside the pastry.

Dried oregano	1 1/4 tsp.	6 mL
Paprika	1 1/4 tsp.	6 mL
Cayenne pepper	1 tsp.	5 mL
Salt	1/2 tsp.	2 mL
Pepper	1 tsp.	5 mL
Garlic powder	1/2 tsp.	2 mL
Onion powder	1/2 tsp.	2 mL
Dried thyme	1/4 tsp.	1 mL
Fine dry bread crumbs	1/2 cup	125 mL
Prepared beef broth	1/4 cup	60 mL
Lean ground beef	1 lb.	454 g
Pastry for three 9 inch (23 cm) pie crusts		
Large egg, fork-beaten	1	1

Combine first 8 ingredients in medium bowl. Reserve 2 tsp. (10 mL) in small cup.

Add bread crumbs and broth to spice mixture in bowl. Stir.

Add beef. Mix well. Divide into 6 equal portions. Roll each portion into 14 inch (35 cm) long log. Chill.

Divide pastry into 3 portions. Roll out 1 portion on lightly floured surface to 6 x 14 inch (15 x 35 cm) rectangle. Cut pastry in half lengthwise. Place 1 beef log along 1 rectangle. Brush opposite long edge with egg. Roll up to enclose filling. Press seam against roll to seal. Repeat with remaining pastry and logs (see Note 1). Brush rolls with egg. Cut each roll into 8 pieces. Arrange, seam-side down, on ungreased baking sheet with sides. Sprinkle with reserved spice mixture. Bake in 400°F (200°C) oven for about 25 minutes until pastry is golden brown and meat thermometer inserted into centre of roll reads 160°F (71°C) (see Note 2). Makes 48 sausage rolls.

1 sausage roll: 89 Calories; 5.2 g Total Fat (0.1 g Mono, 0.1 g Poly, 2.1 g Sat); 13 mg Cholesterol; 8 g Carbohydrate; trace Fibre; 3 g Protein; 95 mg Sodium

Note 1: Unbaked rolls may be stored in airtight container in freezer for up to 3 months. Arrange on ungreased baking sheet with sides. Bake as directed.

(continued on next page)

Rolls, Wraps & Stacks

Note 2: Baked rolls may be stored in airtight container in freezer for up to 3 months. Arrange frozen rolls on ungreased baking sheet with sides. Reheat in 325°F (160°C) oven for 15 to 20 minutes until hot.

Asian Chicken Salad Rolls

Fresh-tasting salad rolls are made even better when they're stuffed with bean sprouts and cilantro. Served up with sweet chili sauce, these will disappear fast!

Rice vermicelli, broken up	2 1/2 oz.	70 g
Boiling water		
Finely chopped cooked chicken	3/4 cup	175 mL
(see Tip, page 140)		
Shredded romaine lettuce, lightly packed	1/2 cup	125 mL
Grated carrot	1/3 cup	75 mL
Chopped fresh bean sprouts	2 tbsp.	30 mL
Chopped fresh cilantro (or parsley)	2 tbsp.	30 mL
Sesame oil (for flavour)	1 tsp.	5 mL
Salt	1/8 tsp.	0.5 mL
Rice paper rounds (6 inch,	16	16
15 cm, diameter)		
Sweet chili sauce	1/2 cup	125 mL

Place vermicelli in small heatproof bowl. Cover with boiling water. Let stand for about 5 minutes until tender. Drain. Rinse with cold water. Drain well. Transfer to medium bowl.

Add next 7 ingredients. Toss.

Place 1 rice paper round in shallow bowl of hot water until just softened. Place on work surface. Spoon about 1/4 cup (60 mL) chicken mixture across centre. Fold sides over filling. Roll up tightly from bottom to enclose filling. Transfer to serving plate. Cover with damp towel to prevent drying. Repeat with remaining rice paper rounds and chicken mixture.

Serve with chili sauce. Makes 16 rolls.

1 roll with 1 1/2 tsp. (7 mL) chili sauce: 292 Calories; 4.0 g Total Fat (0.2 g Mono, 0.1 g Poly, 0.2 g Sat); 6 mg Cholesterol; 63 g Carbohydrate; trace Fibre; 5 g Protein; 787 mg Sodium

Pictured on page 72.

Figs in a Blanket

For the best colour and texture, look for Calimyrna figs. Prepare these ahead of time so all that's left when your guests arrive is popping them in the oven! Garnish with sprigs of fresh thyme just before serving.

Orange juice	1 cup	250 mL
Balsamic vinegar	1/4 cup	60 mL
Granulated sugar	1 tsp.	5 mL
Sprigs of fresh thyme	3	3
Dried figs	24	24
Smoked Gouda cheese cubes (1/2 inch, 12 mm, pieces)	24	24
Prosciutto (or deli ham) slices, cut in half lengthwise	12	12

Combine first 4 ingredients in small saucepan. Bring to a boil. Add figs. Remove from heat. Let stand, covered, for about 15 minutes until figs are plump. Transfer figs with slotted spoon to paper towel-lined plate to drain. Bring vinegar mixture to a boil. Reduce heat to medium. Boil gently, uncovered, for about 8 minutes until reduced to about 1/3 cup (75 mL). Remove and discard thyme sprigs.

Cut 1 inch (2.5 cm) lengthwise slit in each fig. Push 1 cheese cube into each fig. Wrap figs tightly with prosciutto. Secure with wooden picks. Arrange on greased baking sheet with sides. Broil on top rack in oven for about 1 minute until cheese starts to melt. Transfer to serving plate. Drizzle with vinegar mixture. Makes 24 wrapped figs.

1 wrapped fig: 149 Calories; 7.0 g Total Fat (trace Mono, 0.1 g Poly, 4.3 g Sat); 26 mg Cholesterol; 14 g Carbohydrate; 2 g Fibre; 8 g Protein; 360 mg Sodium

Pictured at right.

1. Jerk Chicken Sandwiches, page 62
2. Spanish Cocktail Slices, page 85
3. Figs in a Blanket, above

Rolls, Wraps & Stacks

Pork Jicama Lettuce Wraps

*Present the nicely textured, spicy pork mixture in lettuce "cups" or serve
the lettuce alongside the filling and let your guests serve themselves.
Use the smaller, inner lettuce leaves for best results.*

Cooking oil	1 tsp.	5 mL
Lean ground pork	1 lb.	454 g
Finely grated ginger root	1 tbsp.	15 mL
(or 3/4 tsp., 4 mL, ground ginger)		
Hoisin sauce	1/4 cup	60 mL
Chili paste (sambal oelek)	2 tsp.	10 mL
Garlic cloves, minced	2	2
(or 1/2 tsp., 2 mL, powder)		
Diced jicama	3/4 cup	175 mL
Chopped green onion	1/4 cup	60 mL
Chopped unsalted, roasted cashews	1/4 cup	60 mL
Iceberg lettuce leaves	16	16

Heat cooking oil in large frying pan on medium-high. Add pork. Scramble-fry
for about 8 minutes until no longer pink. Drain. Reduce heat to medium.

Add next 4 ingredients. Heat and stir for 2 minutes. Transfer to medium
bowl. Cool.

Add next 3 ingredients. Stir.

Serve pork mixture with lettuce leaves for wrapping. Makes 16 wraps.

*1 wrap: 85 Calories; 5.3 g Total Fat (2.5 g Mono, 0.6 g Poly,
1.8 g Sat); 19 mg Cholesterol; 4 g Carbohydrate; trace Fibre;
6 g Protein; 164 mg Sodium*

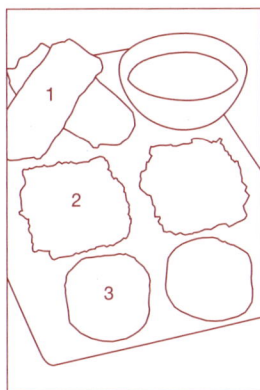

1. Asian Chicken Salad Rolls, page 69
2. Tuna Sushi Stacks, page 84
3. Sesame Shrimp Sushi Rolls, page 74

Curried Chicken Sandwiches

Appetizing triangles with a surprising curried chicken salad and sweet grape filling. The creamy filling can be made up to one day in advance, which will allow the flavour and colour to develop.

Chopped cooked chicken (see Tip, page 140)	1 1/2 cups	375 mL
Chopped red grapes	1/3 cup	75 mL
Mayonnaise	1/3 cup	75 mL
Finely chopped fresh cilantro	2 tbsp.	30 mL
Finely chopped fresh parsley	2 tbsp.	30 mL
Finely chopped green onion	2 tbsp.	30 mL
Curry powder	1 tsp.	5 mL
Salt	1/4 tsp.	1 mL
Pepper	1/8 tsp.	0.5 mL
White (or whole-wheat) sandwich bread slices	16	16

Combine first 9 ingredients in medium bowl.

Arrange 8 bread slices on work surface. Spread filling over top. Cover with remaining bread slices. Trim and discard crusts. Cut each sandwich diagonally into 4 triangles. Makes 32 triangles.

1 triangle: 63 Calories; 3.0 g Total Fat (0.2 g Mono, 0.1 g Poly, 0.6 g Sat); 7 mg Cholesterol; 6 g Carbohydrate; trace Fibre; 3 g Protein; 102 mg Sodium

Sesame Shrimp Sushi Rolls

The sweet potato and cucumber in these neat maki offer delicate flavours and create a healthier appetizer choice. Serve with low-sodium soy sauce mixed with wasabi.

Water	2 1/4 cups	550 mL
Short-grain white rice, rinsed and drained	1 1/2 cups	375 mL
Rice vinegar	2 tbsp.	30 mL
Granulated sugar	1 tbsp.	15 mL
Salt	1/4 tsp.	1 mL

(continued on next page)

Rolls, Wraps & Stacks

Peeled orange-fleshed sweet potato sticks (1/2 x 4 inch, 12 mm x 10 cm, pieces)	8	8
Sesame (or cooking) oil	2 tsp.	10 mL
Nori (roasted seaweed) sheets	4	4
Cooked medium shrimp (peeled and deveined), halved lengthwise	20	20
Sesame and ginger salad dressing	2 tbsp.	30 mL
Julienned English cucumber (with peel), see Tip, below	1/2 cup	125 mL
Roasted sesame seeds	1/4 cup	60 mL

Pour water into small saucepan. Bring to a boil. Add rice. Stir. Reduce heat to medium-low. Simmer, covered, for 20 minutes, without stirring. Remove from heat. Let stand, covered, for about 10 minutes until rice is tender and liquid is absorbed. Transfer to large bowl.

Stir next 3 ingredients in small bowl until sugar is dissolved. Add to rice. Stir. Cool.

Brush both sides of sweet potato with sesame oil. Arrange in greased pie plate. Cook in 425°F (220°C) oven for 10 to 12 minutes until tender-crisp. Cool.

Place 1 nori sheet, shiny-side down, on work surface. Spread about 1 cup (250 mL) rice mixture over nori, leaving 2 inch (5 cm) border on top edge. Place 2 sweet potato sticks across rice mixture, about 2 inches (5 cm) from bottom edge.

Toss shrimp and salad dressing in medium bowl. Arrange 1/4 of shrimp mixture and 1/4 of cucumber beside sweet potato. Sprinkle with 1 tbsp. (15 mL) sesame seeds. Dampen top edge of nori with water. Roll up tightly from bottom to enclose filling. Wrap in plastic wrap. Repeat with remaining ingredients. Chill for about 1 hour until firm. Discard plastic wrap. Trim ends. Cut each roll into 8 slices. Makes 32 rolls.

1 roll: 58 Calories; 1.4 g Total Fat (0.1 g Mono, 0.3 g Poly, 0.1 g Sat); 6 mg Cholesterol; 9 g Carbohydrate; trace Fibre; 2 g Protein; 42 mg Sodium

Pictured on page 72.

tip To julienne, cut into very thin strips that resemble matchsticks.

Thai Chicken Lettuce Wraps

This spicy chicken mix with citrusy lime, crunchy peanuts and fresh cilantro is perfect for wrapping up in crisp lettuce leaves. A delicious do-it-yourself appie that gets your guests in on the action.

Lean ground chicken	1 lb.	454 g
Lime juice	1/4 cup	60 mL
Thinly sliced red onion	1/4 cup	60 mL
Soy sauce	1 tbsp.	15 mL
Finely grated ginger root	2 tsp.	10 mL
(or 1/2 tsp., 2 mL, ground ginger)		
Garlic clove, minced	1	1
(or 1/4 tsp., 1 mL, powder)		
Cooking oil	2 tsp.	10 mL
Chopped fresh cilantro (or parsley)	2 tbsp.	30 mL
Chopped fresh mint	2 tbsp.	30 mL
(or 1 1/2 tsp., 7 mL, dried)		
Chopped green onion	2 tbsp.	30 mL
Chopped salted peanuts, toasted	1 tbsp.	15 mL
(see Tip, page 77)		
Finely diced fresh hot chili pepper	1 tsp.	5 mL
(see Tip, page 115)		
Large green leaf (or butter) lettuce leaves	8	8

Combine first 6 ingredients in medium bowl.

Heat cooking oil in large frying pan on medium. Scramble-fry chicken mixture for about 10 minutes until chicken is no longer pink and liquid is almost evaporated. Transfer to large bowl. Let stand for 5 minutes.

Add next 5 ingredients. Stir.

Serve chicken mixture with lettuce leaves for wrapping. Serves 8.

1 serving: 102 Calories; 6.4 g Total Fat (0.7 g Mono, 0.4 g Poly, 1.5 g Sat); 38 mg Cholesterol; 2 g Carbohydrate; trace Fibre; 10 g Protein; 208 mg Sodium

Rolls, Wraps & Stacks

Blue Cheeseburgers

Mini-burgers are all the rage these days—this version serves up bold blue cheese flavour, nicely complemented by a sweet chutney mayonnaise.

Large egg, fork-beaten	1	1
Crumbled blue cheese	1/4 cup	60 mL
Fine dry bread crumbs	1/4 cup	60 mL
Finely chopped walnuts, toasted (see Tip, below)	1/4 cup	60 mL
Worcestershire sauce	1 tbsp.	15 mL
Pepper	1/2 tsp.	2 mL
Garlic powder	1/4 tsp.	1 mL
Lean ground beef	1 lb.	454 g
Mayonnaise	1/4 cup	60 mL
Mango chutney, chopped	1 tbsp.	15 mL
Mini-buns, split	8	8

Combine first 7 ingredients in large bowl.

Add beef. Mix well. Divide into 8 equal portions. Shape into 2 inch (5 cm) diameter patties. Arrange on greased baking sheet with sides. Broil on top rack in oven for about 3 minutes per side until no longer pink inside.

Combine mayonnaise and chutney in small bowl. Spread over bottom halves of buns. Place patties on mayonnaise mixture. Cover with top halves of buns. Makes 8 burgers.

1 burger: 402 Calories; 26.7 g Total Fat (0.9 g Mono, 1.9 g Poly, 7.3 g Sat); 71 mg Cholesterol; 24 g Carbohydrate; 1 g Fibre; 15 g Protein; 311 mg Sodium

tip When toasting nuts, seeds or coconut, cooking times will vary for each type of nut—so never toast them together. For small amounts, place ingredient in an ungreased shallow frying pan. Heat on medium for 3 to 5 minutes, stirring often, until golden. For larger amounts, spread ingredient evenly in an ungreased shallow pan. Bake in a 350°F (175°C) oven for 5 to 10 minutes, stirring or shaking often, until golden.

Puff Pastry Spirals

Buttery pastries with a bold, flavourful spiral of pesto and olive.
Freezing before slicing helps to keep the slices nicely rounded.

Sun-dried tomato pesto	1/3 cup	75 mL
Finely sliced green onion	2 tbsp.	30 mL
Finely chopped kalamata olives	1 tbsp.	15 mL
Package of puff pastry (14 oz., 397 g), thawed according to package directions	1/2	1/2

Combine first 3 ingredients in small bowl. Roll out puff pastry on lightly floured surface to 8 x 10 inch (20 x 25 cm) rectangle. Spread pesto mixture over pastry, leaving 1/2 inch (12 mm) edge on short sides. Roll up tightly, jelly-roll style, from short side. Pinch seam against roll to seal. Wrap in plastic wrap. Freeze for 30 minutes. Discard plastic wrap. Cut into 1/4 inch (6 mm) slices, using serrated knife. Arrange slices on parchment paper-lined baking sheet with sides. Bake in 425°F (220°C) oven for about 15 minutes until golden. Makes 20 spirals.

1 spiral: 43 Calories; 2.8 g Total Fat (trace Mono, 0 g Poly, 0.7 g Sat); 0 mg Cholesterol; 4 g Carbohydrate; trace Fibre; 1 g Protein; 94 mg Sodium

Chickpea Spinach Samosas

Crisp phyllo makes way for a rich filling of chickpeas and spinach. Hot curry paste could be used instead of the mild if you'd like to spice it up. Be sure to serve these samosas hot from the oven.

Cooking oil	1 tbsp.	15 mL
Chopped fennel bulb (white part only)	3/4 cup	175 mL
Chopped onion	3/4 cup	175 mL
Mild curry paste	1 tbsp.	15 mL
Finely grated ginger root	2 tsp.	10 mL
(or 1/2 tsp., 2 mL, ground ginger)		
Brown sugar, packed	1 tsp.	5 mL
Ground cumin	1/2 tsp.	2 mL
Garlic cloves, minced	2	2
(or 1/2 tsp., 2 mL, powder)		
Salt	1/4 tsp.	1 mL

(continued on next page)

Can of chickpeas (garbanzo beans), rinsed and drained	19 oz.	540 mL
Chopped fresh spinach leaves, lightly packed	1 1/2 cups	375 mL
Frozen peas	1/2 cup	125 mL
Phyllo pastry sheets, thawed according to package directions	10	10
Butter (or hard margarine), melted	1/2 cup	125 mL

Heat cooking oil in large frying pan on medium. Add fennel and onion. Cook for about 12 minutes, stirring often, until fennel and onion are starting to brown.

Add next 6 ingredients. Heat and stir for about 1 minute until fragrant.

Add next 3 ingredients. Heat and stir for about 3 minutes until spinach is wilted.

Place 1 pastry sheet on work surface. Cover remaining sheets with damp towel to prevent drying. Brush with butter. Cut lengthwise into 4 strips. Spoon about 1 tbsp. (15 mL) chickpea mixture onto bottom of strip. Fold 1 corner diagonally towards straight edge to form triangle. Continue folding back and forth to enclose filling (see diagram). Repeat with remaining pastry sheets, butter and chickpea mixture. Arrange on greased baking sheets. Brush with remaining butter (see Note). Bake, 1 sheet at a time, in 375°F (190°C) oven for about 15 minutes until golden. Makes 40 samosas.

1 samosa: 54 Calories; 3.1 g Total Fat (1.0 g Mono, 0.3 g Poly, 1.5 g Sat); 6 mg Cholesterol; 5 g Carbohydrate; 1 g Fibre; 1 g Protein; 85 mg Sodium

Note: Samosas can be frozen uncooked at this point. Brush frozen samosas with butter. Bake in 375°F (190°C) oven for 18 to 20 minutes until golden and heated through.

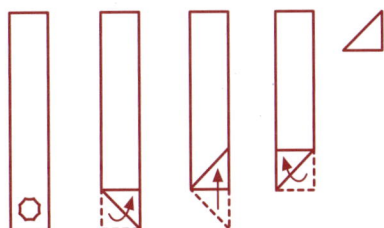

Lemony Chicken Rolls

Inviting phyllo bundles of fresh asparagus and chicken. These may be reheated from chilled in a 375°F (190°C) oven for about 10 minutes until hot.

Cooking oil	1 tsp.	5 mL
Chopped onion	1 cup	250 mL
Chopped fresh asparagus	1 1/2 cups	375 mL
(1/2 inch, 12 mm, pieces)		
Lean ground chicken	1/2 lb.	225 g
Block cream cheese, softened	1/4 cup	60 mL
Lemon juice	2 tbsp.	30 mL
Dried tarragon	1/2 tsp.	2 mL
Grated lemon zest (see Tip, page 93)	1/2 tsp.	2 mL
Salt	1/2 tsp.	2 mL
Phyllo pastry sheets, thawed according	6	6
to package directions		
Butter (or hard margarine), melted	1/3 cup	75 mL

Heat cooking oil in large frying pan on medium. Add onion. Cook for about 5 minutes, stirring often, until softened. Add asparagus. Cook for about 2 minutes until just tender-crisp. Transfer to medium bowl. Let stand for 10 minutes.

Add next 6 ingredients. Mix well.

Layer pastry sheets on work surface. Cut sheets in half crosswise. Stack pieces. Cut in half crosswise, making 24 rectangles. Place 1 rectangle on work surface with short side closest to you. Cover remaining rectangles with damp towel to prevent drying.

Brush with butter. Spoon about 1 1/2 tbsp. (25 mL) chicken mixture along bottom of rectangle, leaving 1 inch (2.5 cm) border on each side. Fold sides over filling. Roll up from bottom to enclose. Place, seam-side down, on greased baking sheet with sides. Cover with separate damp towel. Repeat with remaining pastry rectangles, butter and remaining chicken mixture. Brush tops of rolls with remaining butter. Bake in 400°F (200°C) oven for about 18 minutes until pastry is golden and internal temperature reaches 175°F (80°C). Makes 24 rolls.

1 roll: 64 Calories; 4.6 g Total Fat (1.2 g Mono, 0.2 g Poly, 2.4 g Sat); 16 mg Cholesterol; 4 g Carbohydrate; trace Fibre; 2 g Protein; 102 mg Sodium

Pictured on page 35.

80   Rolls, Wraps & Stacks

Italian Sausage Rolls

Herb-speckled pastry surrounds spicy sausage bites in a filling appetizer that's perfect to serve for an Italian-themed appetizer buffet. Reheat the baked rolls in a 375°F (190°C) oven for 10 minutes until heated through—increase time to 15 minutes if you're reheating them from frozen.

All-purpose flour	1 cup	250 mL
Grated Parmesan cheese	2 tbsp.	30 mL
Dried basil	1/2 tsp.	2 mL
Dried oregano	1/2 tsp.	2 mL
Salt	1/8 tsp.	0.5 mL
Cold butter (or hard margarine), cut up	6 tbsp.	100 mL
Ice water	1/3 cup	75 mL
Mild (or hot) Italian sausage, casing removed	1/2 lb.	225 g
Fine dry bread crumbs	1 tbsp.	15 mL
Large egg, fork-beaten	1	1

Combine first 5 ingredients in medium bowl. Cut in butter until mixture resembles coarse crumbs. Slowly add water, 1 tbsp. (15 mL) at a time, stirring with fork until mixture starts to come together. Do not overmix. Turn out onto lightly floured surface. Shape into flattened disc. Wrap with plastic wrap. Chill for 30 minutes. Roll out pastry on lightly floured surface to 8 x 12 inch (20 x 30 cm) rectangle. Cut crosswise into 3 rectangles.

Combine sausage and bread crumbs in medium bowl. Divide into 3 equal portions. Roll each portion into 8 inch (20 cm) long log. Place 1 sausage log along long side of 1 rectangle. Brush opposite long edge with water. Roll to enclose filling. Press seam against roll to seal. Repeat with remaining pastry and sausage logs.

Brush rolls with egg. Cut each roll into 8 pieces. Using sharp knife, cut small slash across top of each piece. Arrange, seam-side down, on greased baking sheet with sides. Bake in 425°F (220°C) oven for about 15 minutes until pastry is golden and sausage is no longer pink inside. Makes 24 sausage rolls.

1 sausage roll: 74 Calories; 5.2 g Total Fat (0.8 g Mono, 0.1 g Poly, 2.6 g Sat); 22 mg Cholesterol; 4 g Carbohydrate; trace Fibre; 1 g Protein; 139 mg Sodium

Smoked Salmon Roll-ups

Bite-sized rolls feature the classic combo of smoked salmon and cheese with a hint of lemon and chive. These colourful spirals are a delicious party offering and make enough for a crowd.

Spreadable cream cheese	1/2 cup	125 mL
Crumbled feta cheese	3 tbsp.	45 mL
Chopped fresh chives	2 tbsp.	30 mL
(or 1 1/2 tsp., 7 mL, dried)		
Chopped fresh dill (or 3/4 tsp.,	1 tbsp.	15 mL
4 mL, dried)		
Lemon juice	1 tbsp.	15 mL
Pepper	1/4 tsp.	1 mL
Spinach flour tortillas (9 inch,	4	4
23 cm, diameter)		
Smoked salmon slices	7 oz.	200 g
Fresh spinach leaves, lightly packed	2 cups	500 mL

Combine first 6 ingredients in small bowl.

Spread cream cheese mixture over tortillas, leaving 1/2 inch (12 mm) edge. Layer salmon and spinach over cream cheese. Roll up tightly, jelly-roll style. Trim ends. Cut each roll into 8 slices (see Note). Makes 32 roll-ups.

1 roll-up: 48 Calories; 2.5 g Total Fat (0.5 g Mono, 0.1 g Poly, 1.2 g Sat); 6 mg Cholesterol; 4 g Carbohydrate; trace Fibre; 2 g Protein; 130 mg Sodium

Note: For best results, wrap each roll with plastic wrap and chill overnight before slicing.

tip   To crush fennel seed, place in large resealable freezer bag. Seal bag. Gently hit with flat side of meat mallet or with rolling pin.

Cheesy Beef Pockets

You'll find mild, fennel-scented beef filling with tangy sour cream tucked inside these rich, cheesy pastry pockets.

Box of pie crust mix	19 oz.	540 g
Grated sharp Cheddar cheese	1 1/2 cups	375 mL
Cold water	2/3 cup	150 mL
Sour cream	1/2 cup	125 mL
Chopped onion	1/4 cup	60 mL
Dijon mustard	2 tsp.	10 mL
Fennel seed, crushed (see Tip, left)	1/2 tsp.	2 mL
Cayenne pepper	1/8 tsp.	.0.5 mL
Extra-lean ground beef	1/2 lb.	225 g
Large egg, fork-beaten	2	2

Mix pie crust mix and cheese in large bowl, adding water 1 tbsp. (15 mL) at a time, until mixture starts to come together. Do not overmix. Turn out onto lightly floured surface. Divide into 2 equal portions. Shape each portion into ball. Shape into flattened discs. Wrap with plastic wrap. Chill for 30 minutes.

Combine next 5 ingredients in medium bowl.

Add beef. Mix well. Discard plastic wrap from 1 pastry disc. Roll out pastry on lightly floured surface to about 1/8 inch (3 mm) thickness. Cut 12 circles with lightly floured 3 inch (7.5 cm) biscuit cutter. Spoon about 1 tbsp. (15 mL) beef mixture into centre of each circle. Brush edges with egg. Fold over. Press edges together with fork to seal. Repeat with remaining pastry and beef mixture. Arrange pockets on 2 ungreased baking sheets with sides.

Brush tops with egg. Cut 2 small vents in tops of pockets to allow steam to escape. Bake in 375°F (190°C) oven for about 20 minutes until pastry is golden and internal temperature of largest pocket reaches 160°F (71°C). Gently lift pockets with spatula to loosen from baking sheets. Let cool on baking sheets on wire racks for 10 minutes. Makes 24 pockets.

1 pocket: 170 Calories; 10.5 g Total Fat (5.2 g Mono, 1.1 g Poly, 3.7 g Sat); 34 mg Cholesterol; 13 g Carbohydrate; trace Fibre; 6 g Protein; 187 mg Sodium

Pictured on page 107.

Tuna Sushi Stacks

Tuna combines with soy and wasabi for familiar flavours in a unique form.
These fun squares are made with short-grain rice and hold together well.

Water	2 1/4 cups	550 mL
Short-grain white rice, rinsed and drained	1 1/2 cups	375 mL
Rice vinegar	3 tbsp.	45 mL
Granulated sugar	2 tbsp.	30 mL
Roasted sesame seeds	1 tsp.	5 mL
Salt	1/2 tsp.	2 mL
Cans of flaked light tuna (6 oz., 170 g, each), drained	2	2
Grated carrot	1/4 cup	60 mL
Mayonnaise	1/4 cup	60 mL
Finely chopped green onion	2 tbsp.	30 mL
Finely chopped pickled ginger slices	1 tbsp.	15 mL
Soy sauce	1 tbsp.	15 mL
Wasabi paste (Japanese horseradish)	1/2 tsp.	2 mL
Thin radish slices, halved	8	8
Green onion slices, cut diagonally	16	16
Roasted sesame seeds	1 tsp.	5 mL

Pour water into small saucepan. Bring to a boil. Add rice. Stir. Reduce heat to medium-low. Simmer, covered, for 20 minutes, without stirring. Remove from heat. Let stand, covered, for about 10 minutes, until rice is tender and liquid is absorbed. Transfer to large bowl.

Stir next 4 ingredients in small bowl until sugar is dissolved. Add to rice. Stir. Cool.

Combine next 7 ingredients in medium bowl. Line bottom of 9 x 9 inch (23 x 23 cm) pan with foil, leaving 1 inch (2.5 cm) overhang on 2 sides. Press half of rice mixture firmly into pan. Spread tuna mixture evenly over top. Press remaining rice mixture evenly over tuna mixture (see Note). Chill, covered, for 1 hour. Holding foil, remove sushi from pan. Cut with wet knife into 16 squares. Arrange squares on serving plate. Discard foil.

(continued on next page)

Rolls, Wraps & Stacks

Top each square with radish and green onion. Sprinkle with second amount of sesame seeds. Makes 16 stacks.

1 stack: 127 Calories; 3.3 g Total Fat (0.1 g Mono, 0.2 g Poly, 0.5 g Sat); 8 mg Cholesterol; 17 g Carbohydrate; 1 g Fibre; 7 g Protein; 254 mg Sodium

Pictured on page 72.

Note: Use wet hands or plastic wrap set on top of rice to spread rice evenly in pan.

Spanish Cocktail Slices

These hearty slices have zesty, smoky flavour and a bit of spicy heat from chorizo sausage—a satisfying appetizer.

Cooking oil	1 tsp.	5 mL
Chorizo (or hot Italian) sausage, casing removed	1 lb.	454 g
Jar of roasted red peppers, drained, chopped	12 oz.	340 mL
Red wine vinegar	2 tbsp.	30 mL
Liquid honey	1 tbsp.	15 mL
Grated orange zest	1/2 tsp.	2 mL
Block cream cheese, softened	1/4 cup	60 mL
Goat (chèvre) cheese, cut up	2 oz.	57 g
Baguette bread loaf, split	1	1

Heat cooking oil in large saucepan on medium. Add sausage. Scramble-fry for about 5 minutes until no longer pink. Drain.

Add next 4 ingredients. Heat and stir for 1 minute. Remove from heat. Cool.

Add cream cheese and goat cheese. Stir well.

Place baguette halves, cut-side up, on ungreased baking sheet with sides. Spread sausage mixture over top. Press down lightly. Broil on top rack in oven for about 4 minutes until edges are browned. Cut diagonally into 1 1/2 inch (3.8 cm) pieces. Makes about 22 sandwiches.

1 sandwich: 143 Calories; 7.8 g Total Fat (3.0 g Mono, 0.8 g Poly, 3.1 g Sat); 18 mg Cholesterol; 10 g Carbohydrate; trace Fibre; 6 g Protein; 487 mg Sodium

Pictured on page 71.

Vietnamese Sandwich Stacks

Inspired by traditional Vietnamese sandwiches, these small stacks are great for an afternoon picnic or barbecue when something a little more substantial is required.

Rice vinegar	1/3 cup	75 mL
Granulated sugar	2 tbsp.	30 mL
Grated carrot	1/2 cup	125 mL
Grated jicama	1/4 cup	60 mL
Grated radish	1/4 cup	60 mL
Thinly sliced onion	1/4 cup	60 mL
Chopped pickled pepper rings	3 tbsp.	45 mL
Baguette bread loaf, split	1	1
Mayonnaise	1/4 cup	60 mL
Deli ham slices	6	6
Thin slices of English cucumber (with peel)	18	18
Chopped fresh cilantro (or parsley)	2 tbsp.	30 mL

Stir rice vinegar and sugar in small bowl until sugar is dissolved.

Add next 5 ingredients. Stir. Marinate, covered, in refrigerator for 1 hour. Drain. Squeeze carrot mixture to remove excess marinade. Discard any remaining marinade. Return to same small bowl.

Place baguette halves, cut-side up, on ungreased baking sheet. Broil on top rack in oven for about 2 minutes until edges are golden.

Spread mayonnaise over baguette halves.

Arrange ham over mayonnaise on bottom half of loaf. Scatter carrot mixture over ham.

Top with cucumber slices. Sprinkle with cilantro. Cover with top half of loaf. Cut crosswise into 1 1/2 inch (3.8 cm) pieces. Secure with wooden picks. Makes about 12 stacks.

1 stack: 110 Calories; 4.5 g Total Fat (0 g Mono, trace Poly, 0.5 g Sat); 8 mg Cholesterol; 14 g Carbohydrate; 1 g Fibre; 4 g Protein; 297 mg Sodium

Scallops with Lime Sabayon

A classy little number that whips up easily! Just poach the scallops and keep them warm while whisking the sabayon over the poaching liquid. This should be served immediately for best results.

Water	2 cups	500 mL
Dry (or alcohol-free) white wine	1/2 cup	125 mL
Lime juice	2 tsp.	10 mL
Whole black peppercorns	6	6
Bay leaf	1	1
Salt	1/4 tsp.	1 mL
Large sea scallops (see Note)	1 lb.	454 g
LIME SABAYON		
Egg yolks (large)	2	2
Lime juice	2 tbsp.	30 mL
Granulated sugar	1/2 tsp.	2 mL
Salt, sprinkle		
Chopped fresh dill	1/2 tsp.	2 mL
(or 1/8 tsp., 0.5 mL, dried)		

Combine first 6 ingredients in small saucepan. Bring to a boil on medium. Boil gently, uncovered, for 5 minutes to blend flavours.

Add scallops. Stir gently. Cook, uncovered, for about 5 minutes, stirring occasionally, until scallops are opaque. Transfer to serving plate with slotted spoon. Cover to keep warm. Reduce heat to medium-low.

Lime Sabayon: Combine first 4 ingredients in medium heatproof bowl. Set bowl over cooking liquid. Whisk egg yolk mixture for about 4 minutes until thickened enough to leave a path when a spoon runs through it.

Add dill. Stir. Makes about 1/4 cup (60 mL). Spoon over scallops. Discard remaining cooking liquid. Serves 8.

1 serving: 65 Calories; 1.5 g Total Fat (0.5 g Mono, 0.3 g Poly, 0.4 g Sat); 70 mg Cholesterol; 2 g Carbohydrate; trace Fibre; 10 g Protein; 93 mg Sodium

Pictured on page 89.

Note: The crescent-shaped side muscle of a sea scallop can toughen during cooking. To remove it, use your figures or a paring knife to carefully peel it away from the side of the raw scallop.

Buttery Sage Linguine

The simple flavours of buttery pasta with toasty pecans and savoury herbs will awaken your appetite. A lovely starter with sophisticated flavours.

Water	8 cups	2 L
Salt	1 tsp.	5 mL
Linguine	4 oz.	113 g
Butter	1 tbsp.	15 mL
Chopped fresh chives (or green onion)	1 tbsp.	15 mL
Dijon mustard (with whole seeds)	2 tsp.	10 mL
Chopped fresh sage	1 tsp.	5 mL
(or 1/4 tsp., 1 mL, dried)		
Chopped pecans, toasted	1/4 cup	60 mL
(see Tip, page 77)		
Grated Parmesan cheese	1/4 cup	60 mL

Combine water and salt in large saucepan. Bring to a boil. Add pasta. Boil, uncovered, for 9 to 11 minutes, stirring occasionally, until tender but firm. Drain, reserving 1/3 cup (75 mL) cooking water in small bowl. Return pasta to pot.

Add next 4 ingredients and reserved cooking water. Toss. Transfer to 4 serving plates.

Sprinkle with pecans and cheese. Serve immediately. Serves 4.

1 serving: 213 Calories; 10.8 g Total Fat (3.8 g Mono, 1.7 g Poly, 3.4 g Sat); 13 mg Cholesterol; 23 g Carbohydrate; 2 g Fibre; 8 g Protein; 198 mg Sodium

1. Scallops with Lime Sabayon, page 87

Props: Chintz & Company

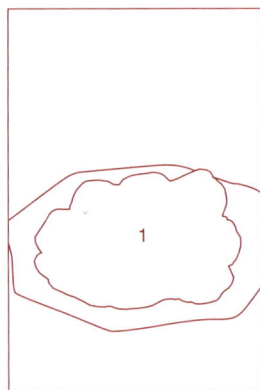

Sit-down Starters

Spicy Shrimp Cocktail

There's a winning combination of fresh flavours and spicy kick in this chilled shrimp cocktail. Your guests are sure to appreciate the clever presentation—olives are always best served in a martini glass!

Chili paste (sambal oelek)	1 tsp.	5 mL
Dried oregano	1/4 tsp.	1 mL
Salt	1/8 tsp.	0.5 mL
Pepper, just a pinch		
Uncooked medium shrimp (peeled and deveined)	1 lb.	454 g
Cooking oil	1 tsp.	5 mL
Chopped sliced green olives	1/2 cup	125 mL
Chopped tomato	1/2 cup	125 mL
Chopped green onion	2 tbsp.	30 mL
Lemon juice	1 tbsp.	15 mL

Combine first 4 ingredients in medium bowl. Add shrimp. Toss.

Heat cooking oil in large frying pan on medium-high. Add shrimp mixture. Cook for about 3 minutes, stirring often, until shrimp turn pink.

Add remaining 4 ingredients. Stir. Transfer to separate medium bowl. Chill. Spoon into 6 martini glasses. Serves 6.

1 serving: 112 Calories; 4.3 g Total Fat (2.3 g Mono, 0.9 g Poly, 0.6 g Sat); 115 mg Cholesterol; 2 g Carbohydrate; 1 g Fibre; 16 g Protein; 881 mg Sodium

1. Shrimp Shooters, page 92
2. Antipasto Salads, page 95

Shrimp Shooters

Unique and surprising—fresh, tangy gazpacho shooters are paired with spicy lime shrimp for an interesting look.

Cooking oil	4 tsp.	20 mL
Chili paste (sambal oelek)	1 1/2 tsp.	7 mL
Grated lime zest (see Tip, right)	1 1/2 tsp.	7 mL
Garlic clove, minced	1	1
(or 1/4 tsp., 1 mL, powder)		
Salt, sprinkle		
Uncooked large shrimp (peeled and deveined), tails intact	16	16
Chopped romaine lettuce, lightly packed	1 1/2 cups	375 mL
Chopped peeled English cucumber	1 cup	250 mL
Chopped fresh cilantro (or parsley)	2 tbsp.	30 mL
Chopped green onion	2 tbsp.	30 mL
Ground cumin	1/8 tsp.	0.5 mL
Salt	1/4 tsp.	1 mL
Pepper	1/8 tsp.	0.5 mL
Finely chopped peeled English cucumber	1/4 cup	60 mL
Finely chopped fresh jalapeño pepper (see Tip, page 115)	1 tsp.	5 mL
Lime juice	1 tsp.	5 mL

Combine first 5 ingredients in medium bowl. Add shrimp. Stir until coated. Marinate, covered, in refrigerator for 30 minutes. Arrange shrimp on greased wire rack set on baking sheet with sides. Discard any remaining marinade. Broil on top rack in oven for 1 to 2 minutes per side until pink. Transfer to small bowl. Chill.

Process next 7 ingredients in blender or food processor until smooth. Transfer to 2 cup (500 mL) measuring cup or pitcher.

Add remaining 3 ingredients. Stir. Chill, covered, for 1 hour. Pour cucumber mixture into 8 shot glasses until 3/4 full (see Note). Hang 2 shrimp on side of each glass. Serves 8.

1 serving: 36 Calories; 2.1 g Total Fat (1.1 g Mono, 0.6 g Poly, 0.2 g Sat); 21 mg Cholesterol; 1 g Carbohydrate; trace Fibre; 3 g Protein; 108 mg Sodium

Pictured on page 90.

Note: Use sherry glasses (with stems) for a more elegant presentation.

Sit-down Starters

Lemon Garlic Mussels

Mussels are always a popular starter—these are bathed in a creamy sauce with a shot of fresh lemon. Serve with plenty of crusty white bread.

Fresh mussels, scrubbed clean (see Note 1)	2 lbs.	900 g
Butter (or hard margarine)	2 tsp.	10 mL
Garlic cloves, minced	2	2
Whipping cream	1 cup	250 mL
Lemon juice	3 tbsp.	45 mL
Dry sherry	2 tbsp.	30 mL
Grated Parmesan cheese	2 tbsp.	30 mL
Grated lemon zest (see Tip, below)	1 tsp.	5 mL
Salt	1/8 tsp.	0.5 mL
Pepper	1/4 tsp.	1 mL

Lightly tap any mussels that are opened 1/4 inch (6 mm) or more. Discard any that do not close (see Note 2).

Melt butter in Dutch oven on medium. Add garlic. Heat and stir for about 1 minute until fragrant.

Add remaining 7 ingredients. Bring to a boil. Add mussels. Cook, covered, for about 6 minutes, stirring once at halftime, until mussels open. Discard any unopened mussels. Transfer mussels with cooking liquid to serving bowl. Serves 4.

1 serving: 301 Calories; 26.3 g Total Fat (7.2 g Mono, 1.3 g Poly, 15.7 g Sat); 106 mg Cholesterol; 7 g Carbohydrate; trace Fibre; 10 g Protein; 388 mg Sodium

Note 1: Remove the "beard," the stringy fibres attached to the shell, either by clipping them or giving them a sharp tug out the hinge end of the mussel (not the open end).

Note 2: For safety reasons, it is important to discard any mussels that do not close before cooking, as well as any that have not opened during cooking.

tip When a recipe calls for grated zest and juice, it's easier to grate the fruit first, then juice it. Be careful not to grate down to the pith (white part of the peel), which is bitter and best avoided.

Chorizo Potato on Kale

Rustic potatoes and sausage are presented on roasted kale for some old-world comfort. Sip on some port or red wine and visit with your guests while you prepare this tapas dish.

Chopped kale leaves, centre ribs removed, lightly packed (see Note 1)	2 cups	500 mL
Olive (or cooking) oil	1 tbsp.	15 mL
Salt	1/4 tsp.	1 mL
Ground nutmeg, sprinkle		
Olive (or cooking) oil	2 tsp.	10 mL
Chorizo (or hot Italian) sausages, sliced	2	2
Chopped onion	1/3 cup	75 mL
Olive (or cooking) oil	1 tsp.	5 mL
Cooked red baby potatoes (see Note 2), cut into 1/4 inch (6 mm) slices	1/2 lb.	225 g
Half-and-half cream	2/3 cup	150 mL
Pine nuts, toasted (see Tip, page 77)	2 tbsp.	30 mL

Toss first 4 ingredients in ungreased 9 x 13 inch (23 x 33 cm) pan. Bake in 400°F (200°C) oven for about 12 minutes until crisp and starting to brown. Arrange on 4 serving plates.

Heat second amount of olive oil in large frying pan on medium. Add sausage and onion. Cook for about 8 minutes, stirring occasionally, until sausage is browned. Transfer to small bowl.

Heat third amount of olive oil in same frying pan. Arrange potato in single layer in pan. Cook for about 4 minutes, turning once, until starting to brown. Add cream and sausage mixture. Stir. Simmer for about 1 minute until cream is thickened. Spoon potato mixture over kale.

Sprinkle with pine nuts. Serves 4.

1 serving: 358 Calories; 26.3 g Total Fat (7.5 g Mono, 2.4 g Poly, 8.1 g Sat); 45 mg Cholesterol; 19 g Carbohydrate; 2 g Fibre; 5 g Protein; 705 mg Sodium

Note 1: To remove the centre rib from lettuce or kale, fold the leaf in half along the rib and then cut along the length of the rib. To store, place leaves in large freezer bag and freeze. Once frozen, crumble in bag.

(continued on next page)

Note 2: Poke holes with fork into potatoes. Microwave, covered, with 1 tbsp. (15 mL) water on high for about 4 minutes until tender but firm (see Tip, page 11). Let stand until cool enough to handle. Cut into 1/4 inch (6 mm) slices.

Antipasto Salads

Bold, rich flavours that are unexpected in a starter salad. Each plate has a colourful and inviting look.

Olive (or cooking) oil	3 tbsp.	45 mL
Balsamic vinegar	2 tbsp.	30 mL
Sun-dried tomato pesto	2 tbsp.	30 mL
Coarsely ground pepper	1/2 tsp.	2 mL
Garlic clove, minced	1	1
(or 1/4 tsp., 1 mL, powder)		
Cubed provolone cheese	1 cup	250 mL
(1/2 inch, 12 mm, pieces)		
Jar of marinated artichoke hearts, drained	6 oz.	170 mL
Sliced red pepper	1/2 cup	125 mL
Genoa salami slices,	2 oz.	57 g
cut into 1/4 inch (6 mm) strips		
Large pitted green olives	1/4 cup	60 mL
Pitted kalamata olives	1/4 cup	60 mL
Shredded romaine lettuce, lightly packed	4 cups	1 L
Chopped fresh basil	2 tbsp.	30 mL
Grape tomatoes, halved lengthwise	9	9

Stir first 5 ingredients in medium bowl until smooth.

Add next 6 ingredients. Toss. Chill, covered, for 2 hours to blend flavours.

Arrange lettuce on 6 serving plates. Spoon cheese mixture over top. Drizzle with any remaining olive oil mixture. Sprinkle with basil. Top with tomato halves. Serves 6.

1 serving: 251 Calories; 19.9 g Total Fat (10.6 g Mono, 1.4 g Poly, 7.3 g Sat); 29 mg Cholesterol; 7 g Carbohydrate; 2 g Fibre; 11 g Protein; 746 mg Sodium

Pictured on page 90.

Orange Sole Pasta Shells

This tasty pasta salad comes with a rather clever presentation—the lovely flavours of sole, fresh veggies and tangy dressing are packed into individual pasta shells for a visual that's truly inspired by the sea.

Water	10 cups	2.5 L
Salt	1 1/2 tsp.	7 mL
Jumbo shell pasta	12	12
Seasoned salt	1/2 tsp.	2 mL
Sole fillets, any small bones removed	3/4 lb.	340 g
Finely chopped red pepper	1/2 cup	125 mL
Finely chopped celery	1/4 cup	60 mL
Orange juice	1/2 cup	125 mL
Finely chopped fresh basil	3 tbsp.	45 mL
Olive (or cooking) oil	3 tbsp.	45 mL
Dijon mustard	2 tsp.	10 mL
Grated orange zest (see Tip, page 93)	1 tsp.	5 mL
Salt	1/2 tsp.	2 mL
Pepper	1/4 tsp.	1 mL

Combine water and salt in Dutch oven or large pot. Bring to a boil. Add pasta shells. Boil, uncovered, for 12 to 14 minutes, stirring occasionally, until tender but firm. Drain. Rinse with cold water. Drain well.

Sprinkle seasoned salt over fillets. Arrange on greased baking sheet with sides. Broil on top rack in oven for about 5 minutes until fish flakes easily when tested with fork. Break into bite-sized pieces. Transfer to medium bowl.

Add red pepper and celery. Stir.

Whisk remaining 7 ingredients in small bowl. Add half of orange juice mixture to fish mixture. Stir. Spoon fish mixture into pasta shells. Transfer to serving plate. Drizzle with remaining orange juice mixture. Makes 12 stuffed shells.

1 stuffed shell: 89 Calories; 4.0 g Total Fat (2.6 g Mono, 0.6 g Poly, 0.6 g Sat); 14 mg Cholesterol; 7 g Carbohydrate; trace Fibre; 6 g Protein; 191 mg Sodium

Shrimp Ceviche

This spicy and smoky tango of citrus and shrimp is perfect for a hot summer night! Serve with crisp pita or tortilla chips.

Cooked shrimp (peeled and deveined), coarsely chopped	1/2 lb.	225 g
Finely chopped red pepper	1/4 cup	60 mL
Finely chopped red onion	2 tbsp.	30 mL
Lime juice	2 tbsp.	30 mL
Olive (or cooking) oil	2 tbsp.	30 mL
Frozen concentrated orange juice, thawed	1 tbsp.	15 mL
Finely chopped chipotle pepper in adobo sauce (see Tip, below)	2 tsp.	10 mL
Ground cumin	1/2 tsp.	2 mL
Salt	1/4 tsp.	1 mL
Diced tomato	1/3 cup	75 mL
Chopped fresh cilantro	2 tbsp.	30 mL

Combine first 9 ingredients in medium bowl. Chill, covered, for 1 hour to blend flavours.

Add tomato and cilantro. Toss gently. Spoon into 4 small dishes. Serves 4.

1 serving: 102 Calories; 7.4 g Total Fat (5.4 g Mono, 0.8 g Poly, 1.1 g Sat); 41 mg Cholesterol; 4 g Carbohydrate; 1 g Fibre; 5 g Protein; 206 mg Sodium

tip Chipotle chili peppers are smoked jalapeño peppers. Be sure to wash your hands after handling. To store any leftover chipotle peppers, divide into recipe-friendly portions and freeze, with sauce, in airtight containers for up to one year.

Gazpacho in Tomato Bowls

Edible tomato bowls make for a fun starter. The gazpacho is tangy with a punch of heat, while the avocado and cilantro cool things down.

Medium tomatoes	6	6
Chopped peeled English cucumber	1/2 cup	125 mL
Chopped red pepper	1/2 cup	125 mL
Chopped fresh cilantro (or parsley)	2 tbsp.	30 mL
Tomato juice	2 tbsp.	30 mL
Chopped green onion	1 tbsp.	15 mL
Lime juice	1 1/2 tsp.	7 mL
Cooking oil	1 tsp.	5 mL
Finely chopped chipotle pepper in adobo sauce (see Tip, page 97)	1/4 tsp.	1 mL
Ground cumin	1/4 tsp.	1 mL
Smoked (sweet) paprika	1/4 tsp.	1 mL
Garlic clove, chopped (or 1/8 tsp., 0.5 mL, powder)	1	1
Salt	1/8 tsp.	0.5 mL
Fine dry bread crumbs	1 tsp.	5 mL
Diced avocado	1/4 cup	60 mL
Lime juice	1/2 tsp.	2 mL
Sprigs of fresh cilantro (or parsley), for garnish	6	6

Slice 1/2 inch (12 mm) from top of each tomato. Discard slices. Using small spoon, remove seeds and pulp, leaving 1/4 inch (6 mm) shell. Reserve 3/4 cup (175 mL) seeds and pulp in small cup. Place tomato shells, cut-side down, on paper towel-lined plate. Chill.

Process next 12 ingredients and reserved seeds and pulp in blender or food processor until smooth. Transfer to medium bowl.

Add bread crumbs. Stir. Chill, covered, for 2 hours to blend flavours. Place tomato shells, cut-side up, on 6 serving plates. If necessary, remove thin slice from bottom of tomato shells so they will stand upright. Fill with cucumber mixture.

Toss avocado and lime juice in small bowl. Spoon over cucumber mixture.

(continued on next page)

Garnish with cilantro sprigs. Serves 6.

1 serving: 53 Calories; 2.1 g Total Fat (1.1 g Mono, 0.6 g Poly, 0.3 g Sat); 0 mg Cholesterol; 8 g Carbohydrate; 3 g Fibre; 2 g Protein; 75 mg Sodium

Goat Cheese Pecan Salad

The refined flavours of creamy goat cheese and mandarin oranges blend wonderfully for a deliciously sweet and savoury salad. Toasting the pecans also brings out their robust flavour.

Mixed salad greens, lightly packed	8 cups	2 L
Fresh orange segments, halved (see Note)	1 cup	250 mL
Chopped pecans, toasted (see Tip, page 77)	3/4 cup	175 mL
Goat (chèvre) cheese, cut up	4 oz.	113 g
ORANGE VINAIGRETTE		
Cooking oil	3 tbsp.	45 mL
Orange juice	2 tbsp.	30 mL
Apple cider vinegar	1 tbsp.	15 mL
Liquid honey	1 tbsp.	15 mL
Dijon mustard	1 tsp.	5 mL
Grated orange zest (see Tip, page 93)	1/2 tsp.	2 mL
Salt	1/8 tsp.	0.5 mL
Coarsely ground pepper	1/8 tsp.	0.5 mL

Toss first 4 ingredients in large bowl.

Orange Vinaigrette: Whisk all 8 ingredients in small bowl. Makes about 1/2 cup (125 mL). Drizzle over greens mixture. Toss. Makes about 11 cups (2.75 L).

1 cup (250 mL): 149 Calories; 12.9 g Total Fat (6.3 g Mono, 3.0 g Poly, 2.9 g Sat); 8 mg Cholesterol; 6 g Carbohydrate; 2 g Fibre; 4 g Protein; 96 mg Sodium

Note: To segment citrus, trim a small slice of peel from both ends so the flesh is exposed. Place the fruit, cut-side down, on a cutting board. Remove the peel with a sharp knife, cutting down and around the flesh, leaving as little pith as possible. Over a small bowl, cut on either side of the membranes to release the segments.

Tuscan Terrine

A rustic terrine with Italian-inspired garlic and sun-dried tomato flavours.
Serve over lightly dressed fresh greens or with a roasted red pepper sauce.

Egg white (large)	1	1
Boneless, skinless chicken thighs, coarsely chopped	1 lb.	454 g
Pine nuts, toasted (see Tip, page 77)	1/4 cup	60 mL
Sun-dried tomatoes, softened in boiling water for 10 minutes before chopping	1/4 cup	60 mL
Whipping cream	1/4 cup	60 mL
Sun-dried tomato pesto	2 tbsp.	30 mL
Garlic clove, minced (or 1/4 tsp., 1 mL, powder)	1	1
Salt	1/2 tsp.	2 mL
Pepper	1/4 tsp.	1 mL
Lean ground chicken	1/2 lb.	225 g

Line greased 9 x 5 x 3 inch (23 x 12.5 x 7.5 cm) loaf pan with parchment paper, allowing paper to extend about 1 inch (2.5 cm) over sides of pan. Combine first 9 ingredients in large bowl.

Add ground chicken. Mix well. Spread evenly in prepared pan. Fold parchment paper over chicken mixture. Cover with foil. Place wire rack in bottom of large roasting pan. Pour boiling water into roasting pan until about 1 inch (2.5 cm) deep. Set loaf pan on wire rack. Cook in 325°F (160°C) oven for about 1 1/2 hours until internal temperature of terrine reaches 175°F (80°C). Transfer to wire rack to cool. Discard foil. Drain and discard any excess liquid and fat. Using parchment paper, lift terrine out of pan. Invert onto plate. Discard parchment paper. Chill, covered, for 6 hours or overnight. Cuts into fourteen 1/2 inch (12 mm) slices.

1 slice: 106 Calories; 5.6 g Total Fat (1.5 g Mono, 1.2 g Poly, 1.8 g Sat); 31 mg Cholesterol;
2 g Carbohydrate; trace Fibre; 9 g Protein; 146 mg Sodium

Spicy Roasted Pepper Soup

Versatile for entertaining, this puréed soup with red pepper sweetness and warming chipotle heat can be served hot or chilled. Creamy buttermilk provides the perfect contrast for the smoky, sweet flavours of roasted red pepper.

Cooking oil	1 tsp.	5 mL
Sliced leek (white part only)	1 cup	250 mL
Chopped celery	1/2 cup	125 mL
Dried basil	1/2 tsp.	2 mL
Garlic clove, minced (or 1/4 tsp., 1 mL, powder)	1	1
Salt	1/4 tsp.	1 mL
Pepper	1/4 tsp.	1 mL
Prepared chicken broth	3 cups	750 mL
Chopped roasted red pepper	1 1/2 cups	375 mL
Granulated sugar	1 1/2 tsp.	7 mL
Finely chopped chipotle peppers in adobo sauce (see Tip, page 97)	1/2 tsp.	2 mL
Buttermilk	1/2 cup	125 mL

Heat cooking oil in large saucepan on medium. Add leek and celery. Cook for about 8 minutes, stirring often, until leek is golden and celery starts to soften.

Add next 4 ingredients. Heat and stir for about 1 minute until garlic is fragrant.

Add next 4 ingredients. Stir. Bring to a boil. Reduce heat to medium-low. Simmer, covered, for about 15 minutes until celery is soft. Carefully process with hand blender or in blender until smooth (see Safety Tip).

Add buttermilk. Stir. Makes about 5 cups (1.25 L).

3/4 cup (175 mL): 84 Calories; 1.7 g Total Fat (0.7 g Mono, 0.4 g Poly, 0.4 g Sat); 1 mg Cholesterol; 10 g Carbohydrate; trace Fibre; 4 g Protein; 755 mg Sodium

Safety Tip: Follow manufacturer's instructions for processing hot liquids.

Black Bean Jalapeño Nachos

A big dish of loaded nachos is just the ticket for a casual get-together. These have a spicy jalapeño kick, and are great served with sour cream and salsa.

Cooking oil	1 tsp.	5 mL
Chopped onion	1 cup	250 mL
Can of black beans, rinsed and drained	19 oz.	540 mL
Chili powder	1 tsp.	5 mL
Ground cumin	1/2 tsp.	2 mL
Garlic clove, minced	1	1
(or 1/4 tsp., 1 mL, powder)		
Salt	1/8 tsp.	0.5 mL
Chopped avocado	1/2 cup	125 mL
Chopped orange pepper	1/2 cup	125 mL
Chopped green onion	1/4 cup	60 mL
Chopped sliced pickled jalapeño pepper	1/4 cup	60 mL
Bag of tortilla chips	11 1/2 oz.	320 g
Grated Mexican cheese blend	2 cups	500 mL

Heat cooking oil in large frying pan on medium. Add onion. Cook for about 5 minutes, stirring often, until softened. Add next 5 ingredients. Heat and stir for about 2 minutes until garlic is fragrant.

Toss next 4 ingredients in small bowl.

To assemble, layer ingredients in ungreased 9 x 13 inch (23 x 33 cm) baking dish as follows:

1. Half of tortilla chips
2. Half of bean mixture
3. Half of avocado mixture
4. Half of cheese
5. Remaining tortilla chips
6. Remaining bean mixture
7. Remaining avocado mixture
8. Remaining cheese

Bake in 400°F (200°C) oven for about 10 minutes until cheese is melted. Serves 8.

(continued on next page)

Sit-down Starters

1 serving: 399 Calories; 21.1 g Total Fat (5.2 g Mono, 5.0 g Poly, 6.3 g Sat); 25 mg Cholesterol; 40 g Carbohydrate; 7 g Fibre; 13 g Protein; 607 mg Sodium

Baked Dill Calamari

Finally, a more approachable calamari recipe—no deep fryer required! Baking creates a nice crisp coating with dill, garlic and a hint of spice.

Fine dry bread crumbs	1 1/2 cups	375 mL
Dried dillweed	1 tsp.	5 mL
Garlic powder	1/2 tsp.	2 mL
Lemon pepper	1/2 tsp.	2 mL
Salt	1/2 tsp.	2 mL
Cayenne pepper	1/8 tsp.	0.5 mL
Large egg	1	1

Small squid tubes, cut into
  1/2 inch (12 mm) rings, rinsed
  and drained
	1 lb.	454 g

Cooking spray		
Finely chopped red onion, for garnish		
Lemon wedges, for garnish		

Combine first 6 ingredients in large resealable freezer bag.

Beat egg with fork in small shallow bowl. Dip squid into egg. Add to bread crumb mixture. Seal bag. Toss until coated. Discard any remaining egg and bread crumb mixture. Arrange squid on greased baking sheet with sides.

Spray with cooking spray. Bake in 425°F (220°C) oven for about 10 minutes, stirring once at halftime, until golden. Transfer to serving dish.

Sprinkle with onion. Serve with lemon wedges. Makes about 4 cups (1 L).

1/2 cup (125 mL): 146 Calories; 2.7 g Total Fat (0.3 g Mono, 0.4 g Poly, 0.4 g Sat); 159 mg Cholesterol; 16 g Carbohydrate; 1 g Fibre; 13 g Protein; 357 mg Sodium

Fennel Radicchio Slaw

Treat your guests to a nutritious appetizer with loads of visual appeal—this colourful and interesting combination of vegetables and apricot is all dressed up in an apple cider vinaigrette. Arrange the slaw over the butter lettuce leaves just before serving.

Apple cider vinegar	2 tbsp.	30 mL
Cooking oil	1 tbsp.	15 mL
Granulated sugar	1 tsp.	5 mL
Salt	1/8 tsp.	0.5 mL
Pepper, just a pinch		
Thinly sliced fennel bulb (white part only)	1 1/2 cups	375 mL
Grated carrot	1/2 cup	125 mL
Thinly sliced radicchio	1/2 cup	125 mL
Finely chopped dried apricot	1/4 cup	60 mL
Chopped fresh chives	1 tbsp.	15 mL
Butter lettuce leaves	4	4

Whisk first 5 ingredients in medium bowl.

Add next 5 ingredients. Toss until coated.

Arrange lettuce leaves on 4 serving plates. Spoon fennel mixture over lettuce. Serves 4.

1 serving: 73 Calories; 3.6 g Total Fat (2.1 g Mono, 1.1 g Poly, 0.3 g Sat); 0 mg Cholesterol; 10 g Carbohydrate; 2 g Fibre; 1 g Protein; 108 mg Sodium

Hummus Roast Vegetable Plate

Roasting vegetables brings out their natural sweetness—a perfect match for lemony hummus. If you'd like to make your own hummus, try our Sesame Seed Hummus, page 24, but skip the lemon juice and parsley called for below.

Prepared hummus	1 cup	250 mL
Chopped fresh parsley	1 tbsp.	15 mL
(or 3/4 tsp., 4 mL, flakes)		
Lemon juice	2 tsp.	10 mL
Balsamic vinegar	2 tbsp.	30 mL
Olive (or cooking) oil	2 tbsp.	30 mL
Granulated sugar	1 tsp.	5 mL
Salt	1/8 tsp.	0.5 mL
Pepper	1/8 tsp.	0.5 mL
Asian eggplant slices (with peel), cut diagonally (about 1/2 inch, 12 mm, each)	6	6
Small zucchini slices (with peel), cut diagonally (about 1/2 inch, 12 mm, each)	6	6
Large orange pepper, cut lengthwise into 6 wedges	1	1
Large red pepper, cut lengthwise into 6 wedges	1	1

Combine first 3 ingredients in small bowl. Set aside.

Combine next 5 ingredients in large bowl.

Add remaining 4 ingredients. Stir until coated. Arrange in single layer on greased baking sheet with sides. Cook in 450°F (230°C) oven for about 20 minutes, turning once at halftime, until browned. Arrange vegetables on 6 serving plates. Spoon hummus mixture over top. Serves 6.

1 serving: 140 Calories; 8.9 g Total Fat (5.3 g Mono, 2.0 g Poly, 1.3 g Sat); 0 mg Cholesterol; 13 g Carbohydrate; 4 g Fibre; 4 g Protein; 212 mg Sodium

Lamb Chops with Mint Pesto

These delicate lamb chops are an elegant first course—fresh mint pesto is a vibrant accompaniment.

Lamb loin chops (about 1 1/2 lbs., 680 g)	8	8
Salt, sprinkle		
Pepper, sprinkle		
Fresh mint leaves, lightly packed	1/2 cup	125 mL
Fresh parsley leaves, lightly packed	1/4 cup	60 mL
Pine nuts, toasted (see Tip, page 77)	1/4 cup	60 mL
Grated Parmesan cheese	2 tbsp.	30 mL
Olive (or cooking) oil	2 tbsp.	30 mL
White wine vinegar	2 tbsp.	30 mL
Liquid honey	1 tsp.	5 mL
Garlic clove, chopped	1	1
(or 1/4 tsp., 1 mL, powder)		
Salt	1/4 tsp.	1 mL

Sprinkle lamb with salt and pepper. Arrange on greased wire rack set on baking sheet with sides. Broil on centre rack in oven for about 8 minutes per side until internal temperature reaches 145°F (63°C) for medium-rare or until lamb reaches desired doneness. Cover with foil. Let stand for 5 minutes. Transfer to serving plate.

Process remaining 9 ingredients in blender until smooth. Spoon over lamb. Serves 8.

1 serving: 228 Calories; 18.3 g Total Fat (8.3 g Mono, 2.6 g Poly, 5.8 g Sat); 50 mg Cholesterol; 2 g Carbohydrate; trace Fibre; 14 g Protein; 143 mg Sodium

1. Sweet and Smoky Nut Mix, page 50
2. Rosemary Olives and Feta, page 41
3. Cheesy Beef Pockets, page 83

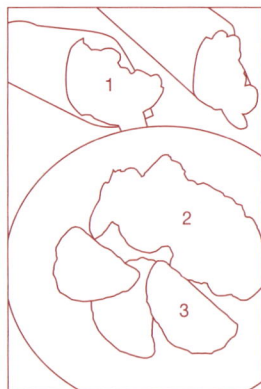

Grilled Fruit Kabobs

Enjoy sweet summer fruit with a smoky grilled flavour in this unexpected starter—grilling caramelizes the natural sugars and intensifies the flavour. An easy addition to a barbecued meal! Choose firm fruit that is just ripe.

Liquid honey	1/4 cup	60 mL
Cooking oil	1 tbsp.	15 mL
Lime juice	1 tbsp.	15 mL
Finely grated ginger root	1 tsp.	5 mL
(or 1/4 tsp., 1 mL, ground ginger)		
Ground cinnamon	1/4 tsp.	1 mL
Salt, sprinkle		
Honeydew cubes (1 inch, 2.5 cm, pieces)	12	12
Cantaloupe cubes (1 inch, 2.5 cm, pieces)	12	12
Pineapple cubes (1 inch, 2.5 cm, pieces)	12	12
Small fresh strawberries	12	12
Bamboo skewers (8 inches, 20 cm, each), soaked in water for 10 minutes	12	12

Whisk first 6 ingredients in small bowl.

Thread next 4 ingredients onto skewers. Brush with honey mixture. Preheat gas barbecue to medium-high. Arrange skewers on greased grill. Close lid. Cook for about 2 minutes per side, brushing occasionally with honey mixture, until dark grill marks appear. Makes 12 skewers.

1 skewer: 55 Calories; 1.3 g Total Fat (0.7 g Mono, 0.4 g Poly, 0.1 g Sat); 0 mg Cholesterol; 11 g Carbohydrate; 1 g Fibre; trace Protein; 6 mg Sodium

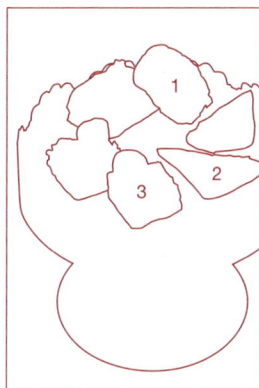

1. Baklava Bundles, page 150
2. Caramelized Apple Samosas, page 148
3. Raspberry Hazelnut Brownies, page 151
Props: HomeSense

Mango Veggie Skewers

Appetizing skewers are loaded with smoky grilled flavour and a punch of curry heat. This vegetarian option has the added benefit of being low in carbohydrates.

Curry paste	1 tbsp.	15 mL
Finely grated ginger root	1 tbsp.	15 mL
(or 3/4 tsp., 4 mL, ground ginger)		
Sesame oil (for flavour)	1 tbsp.	15 mL
Grated lemon zest	1 tsp.	5 mL
Chili paste (sambal oelek)	1/2 tsp.	2 mL
Garlic clove, minced	1	1
(or 1/4 tsp., 1 mL, powder)		
Large frozen mango pieces	16	16
Small fresh whole white mushrooms	16	16
Small zucchini slices (with peel), about	16	16
1/2 inch (12 mm) each		
Large red pepper, cut into 16 pieces	1	1
Bamboo skewers (8 inches, 20 cm, each),	16	16
soaked in water for 10 minutes		

Combine first 6 ingredients in medium bowl.

Add next 4 ingredients. Toss until coated. Marinate, covered, in refrigerator for 30 minutes, stirring occasionally.

Thread mango and vegetables onto skewers. Reserve any remaining curry paste mixture. Preheat gas barbecue to medium. Arrange skewers on greased grill. Close lid. Cook for about 3 minutes per side, brushing with curry paste mixture, until red pepper is tender-crisp. Makes 16 skewers.

1 skewer: 23 Calories; 1.0 g Total Fat (trace Mono, 0.1 g Poly, 0.2 g Sat); 0 mg Cholesterol; 4 g Carbohydrate; 1 g Fibre; 1 g Protein; 35 mg Sodium

Pictured on page 36 and on back cover.

Sweet and Sour Tofu Skewers

These saucy skewers feature tender tofu and colourful, toothsome vegetables,
infused with sweet-and-sour flavour.

Brown sugar, packed	1/2 cup	125 mL
Rice vinegar	1/2 cup	125 mL
Tomato paste (see Tip, below)	3 tbsp.	45 mL
Soy sauce	2 tbsp.	30 mL
Water	2 tbsp.	30 mL
Cornstarch	2 tsp.	10 mL
Package of firm tofu, cut into 36 cubes	10.7 oz.	300 g
Canned whole baby corn, blotted dry, halved crosswise	9	9
Broccoli florets	18	18
Large red pepper, cut into 18 pieces	1	1
Bamboo skewers (6 inches, 15 cm, each), soaked in water for 10 minutes	18	18

Whisk first 6 ingredients in small saucepan. Bring to a boil. Reduce heat to medium. Heat and stir for about 2 minutes until boiling and thickened.

Thread next 4 ingredients onto skewers. Arrange on greased baking sheet with sides. Brush both sides with brown sugar mixture. Broil on centre rack in oven for 8 to 12 minutes until broccoli and red pepper are tender-crisp. Brush with remaining brown sugar mixture. Makes 18 skewers.

1 skewer: 44 Calories; 0.4 g Total Fat (0.1 g Mono, 0.2 g Poly, 0.1 g Sat); 0 mg Cholesterol;
9 g Carbohydrate; 1 g Fibre; 2 g Protein; 163 mg Sodium

tip   If a recipe calls for less than an entire can of tomato paste, freeze the unopened can for 30 minutes. Open both ends and push the contents through one end. Slice off only what you need. Freeze the remaining paste in a resealable freezer bag or plastic wrap for future use.

Korean BBQ Beef Skewers

The addictively sweet and spicy flavour of Korean barbecue in a satay-style skewer. The bite-sized beef is deliciously marinated.

Brown sugar, packed	1/4 cup	60 mL
Soy sauce	1/4 cup	60 mL
Rice vinegar	3 tbsp.	45 mL
Finely grated ginger root	1 tbsp.	15 mL
Garlic cloves, minced	3	3
Sesame oil (for flavour)	1 tbsp.	15 mL
Pepper	1/4 tsp.	1 mL
Thick sirloin steak, cut across grain into 1/8 inch (3 mm) slices (see Tip, below)	1 1/2 lbs.	680 g
Bamboo skewers (8 inches, 20 cm, each), soaked in water for 10 minutes	12	12

Combine first 7 ingredients in medium bowl.

Add beef. Stir until coated. Marinate, covered, in refrigerator for 30 minutes, stirring occasionally.

Thread beef, accordion-style, onto skewers. Discard any remaining marinade. Preheat gas barbecue to medium. Arrange skewers on greased grill. Cook for about 2 minutes per side until no longer pink. Makes 12 skewers.

1 skewer: 100 Calories; 4.5 g Total Fat (1.6 g Mono, 0.2 g Poly, 1.6 g Sat); 30 mg Cholesterol; 2 g Carbohydrate; trace Fibre; 12 g Protein; 190 mg Sodium

tip To slice meat easily, place in freezer for about 30 minutes until just starting to freeze. If using from frozen state, partially thaw before cutting.

Smoky Bacon-wrapped Shrimp

The natural sweetness of lemony-spiced shrimp is complemented by smoky bacon. These will go fast—you can't go wrong with bacon at a party!

Bacon slices	12	12
Cooking oil	2 tbsp.	30 mL
Grated lemon zest	1/2 tsp.	2 mL
Smoked (sweet) paprika	1/2 tsp.	2 mL
Garlic clove, minced	1	1
(or 1/4 tsp., 1 mL, powder)		
Pepper	1/4 tsp.	1 mL
Hot pepper sauce	1/8 tsp.	0.5 mL
Uncooked large shrimp	12	12
(peeled and deveined)		
Bamboo skewers (4 inches, 10 cm, each),	12	12
soaked in water for 10 minutes		

Cook bacon, in 2 batches, in large frying pan on medium for about 4 minutes per side until starting to brown but still flexible. Transfer to paper towel-lined plate to drain. Let stand until cool enough to handle.

Combine next 6 ingredients in small bowl. Add shrimp. Toss.

Wrap 1 slice of bacon around each shrimp. Secure with skewer. Preheat gas barbecue to medium-high. Arrange skewers on greased grill. Cook for about 2 minutes per side until bacon is crisp and shrimp are pink. Makes 12 bacon-wrapped shrimp.

1 bacon-wrapped shrimp: 63 Calories; 5.1 g Total Fat (2.6 g Mono, 1.1 g Poly, 1.1 g Sat); 18 mg Cholesterol; trace Carbohydrate; trace Fibre; 4 g Protein; 158 mg Sodium

California Sushi Skewers

These unwrapped California sushi rolls create simple, attractive skewers served with wasabi-spiked soy sauce. For best results, choose avocados that are ripe but firm.

Water	3/4 cup	175 mL
Short-grain white rice, rinsed and drained	1/3 cup	75 mL
Granulated sugar	2 tsp.	10 mL
Rice vinegar	2 tsp.	10 mL
Salt	1/8 tsp.	0.5 mL
Nori (roasted seaweed) sheets, cut into eighteen 1/2 x 3 inch (12 mm x 7.5 cm) strips	2	2
Avocado cubes (3/4 inch, 2 cm, pieces)	18	18
Lemon juice	1 tbsp.	15 mL
Cooked large shrimp (peeled and deveined)	18	18
English cucumber (with peel), quartered and cut into eighteen 3/4 inch (2 cm) pieces	1/4	1/4
Bamboo skewers (8 inches, 20 cm, each)	18	18
Soy sauce	1/2 cup	125 mL
Wasabi paste	1/2 tsp.	2 mL

Pour water into small saucepan. Bring to a boil. Add rice. Stir. Reduce heat to medium-low. Simmer, covered, for 12 minutes, without stirring. Remove from heat. Let stand, covered, for about 10 minutes until rice is tender and liquid is absorbed. Transfer to medium bowl.

Stir next 3 ingredients in small cup until sugar is dissolved. Add to rice. Stir. Cool. Roll into eighteen 3/4 inch (2 cm) balls.

Wrap strip of nori around each rice ball. Chill, covered, for about 1 hour until firm.

Gently toss avocado and lemon juice in medium bowl.

Thread avocado, shrimp, cucumber and rice balls onto skewers.

(continued on next page)

Sticks & Skewers

Whisk soy sauce and wasabi in small bowl. Serve with skewers. Makes 18 skewers.

1 skewer with 1 1/2 tsp. (7 mL) soy sauce mixture: 39 Calories; 1.2 g Total Fat (0.7 g Mono, 0.2 g Poly, 0.2 g Sat); 11 mg Cholesterol; 5 g Carbohydrate; 1 g Fibre; 2 g Protein; 620 mg Sodium

Pictured on page 125.

Margarita Shrimp

Cocktail shrimp bursting with the sweet and tangy tropical-inspired flavours of lime, cilantro and tequila! A fun appetizer to serve at cocktail hour.

Chopped fresh cilantro	1/4 cup	60 mL
Orange juice	1/4 cup	60 mL
Lime juice	3 tbsp.	45 mL
Tequila	2 tbsp.	30 mL
Finely chopped fresh jalapeño pepper (see Tip, below)	1 tbsp.	15 mL
Granulated sugar	2 tsp.	10 mL
Grated lime zest (see Tip, page 93)	1 tsp.	5 mL
White vinegar	1 tsp.	5 mL
Grated orange zest (see Tip, page 93)	1/2 tsp.	2 mL
Salt	1/4 tsp.	1 mL
Cooked large shrimp (peeled and deveined), about 1 lb. (454 g)	34	34
Cocktail picks	34	34

Combine first 10 ingredients in large bowl.

Add shrimp. Chill, covered, for 4 hours to blend flavours. Transfer shrimp mixture to serving dish. Insert cocktail picks into shrimp. Makes 34 shrimp.

1 shrimp: 18 Calories; 0.2 g Total Fat (trace Mono, 0.1 g Poly, trace Sat); 26 mg Cholesterol; 1 g Carbohydrate; trace Fibre; 3 g Protein; 47 mg Sodium

Pictured on page 17.

tip Hot peppers contain capsaicin in the seeds and ribs. Removing the seeds and ribs will reduce the heat. Wear rubber gloves when handling hot peppers and avoid touching your eyes. Wash your hands well afterwards.

Maple Salmon Sticks

Salmon pairs so well with sweet flavours—here, peppery salmon combines
with maple syrup sweetness.

Maple syrup	1/2 cup	125 mL
Soy sauce	2 tbsp.	30 mL
Brown sugar, packed	1 tbsp.	15 mL
Pepper	1/8 tsp.	0.5 mL
Salmon fillets, skin removed, cut into twenty 1/2 inch (12 mm) strips	1 lb.	454 g
Bamboo skewers (8 inches, 20 cm, each) soaked in water for 10 minutes	20	20

Combine first 4 ingredients in small bowl. Place salmon in large resealable freezer bag. Pour maple syrup mixture over top. Seal bag. Marinate in refrigerator for 6 hours or overnight, turning occasionally. Remove salmon. Discard any remaining marinade. Transfer remaining maple syrup mixture to small saucepan. Bring to a boil. Reduce heat to medium. Boil gently for about 5 minutes until reduced to about 3 tbsp. (45 mL).

Thread salmon onto ends of skewers. Arrange in alternating pattern on greased foil-lined baking sheet with sides (see Note). Broil on top rack in oven for about 3 minutes until fish flakes easily when tested with fork. Brush with maple syrup mixture. Makes 20 skewers.

1 skewer: 56 Calories; 1.5 g Total Fat (0.5 g Mono, 0.6 g Poly, 0.2 g Sat); 12 mg Cholesterol;
6 g Carbohydrate; 0 g Fibre; 5 g Protein; 142 mg Sodium

Note: Arranging the skewers with the stick ends on alternating sides of the baking sheet will insulate the skewers and reduce scorching.

Shrimp Artichoke Skewers

For a light appetizer, try these simple skewers of mildly spiced shrimp and tangy artichoke, complete with great smoky flavour from the grill.

Reserved liquid from artichokes	2/3 cup	150 mL
Chopped fresh basil	2 tsp.	10 mL
(or 1/2 tsp., 2 mL, dried)		
Chili paste (sambal oelek)	1 tsp.	5 mL
Garlic clove, minced	1	1
(or 1/4 tsp., 1 mL, powder)		
Uncooked large shrimp	32	32
(peeled and deveined)		
Jar of marinated artichoke hearts,	12 oz.	341 mL
drained and liquid reserved		
Bamboo skewers (8 inches, 20 cm, each),	16	16
soaked in water for 10 minutes		

Combine first 4 ingredients in medium bowl. Reserve 1/4 cup (60 mL) in small cup.

Add shrimp to remaining artichoke mixture. Toss until coated. Marinate, covered, in refrigerator for 30 minutes. Remove shrimp. Discard any remaining marinade.

Cut larger artichokes in half to make 16 pieces. Thread 2 shrimp and 1 artichoke onto each skewer. Preheat gas barbecue to medium. Arrange skewers on greased grill. Close lid. Cook for 2 to 3 minutes per side, brushing with reserved artichoke mixture, until shrimp turn pink. Makes 16 skewers.

1 skewer: 23 Calories; 0.2 g Total Fat (trace Mono, 0.1 g Poly, 0.1 g Sat); 21 mg Cholesterol; 2 g Carbohydrate; trace Fibre; 3 g Protein; 79 mg Sodium

Donair Kabobs

Those popular donair flavours are combined on a simple skewer. Lamb meatballs are paired with tomato, onion and mint for a sure-fire favourite.

Large egg, fork-beaten	1	1
Fine dry bread crumbs	1/3 cup	75 mL
Finely chopped onion	2 tbsp.	30 mL
Chopped fresh mint (or 1/2 tsp., 2 mL, dried)	2 tsp.	10 mL
White vinegar	1 tsp.	5 mL
Ground cumin	1/2 tsp.	2 mL
Garlic clove, minced (or 1/4 tsp., 1 mL, powder)	1	1
Salt	1/4 tsp.	1 mL
Pepper	1/4 tsp.	1 mL
Lean ground lamb	3/4 lb.	340 g
Fresh mint leaves	24	24
Red onion pieces (1 inch, 2.5 cm, each), separated into layers	24	24
Small tomatoes, cut into 8 wedges each	3	3
Bamboo skewers (4 inches, 10 cm, each)	24	24

Combine first 9 ingredients in large bowl.

Add lamb. Mix well. Roll into 24 balls, using about 1 tbsp. (15 mL) for each. Arrange in single layer on greased baking sheet with sides. Cook in 400°F (200°C) oven for about 13 minutes until no longer pink inside.

Thread meatballs and remaining 3 ingredients, in order given, onto skewers. Makes 24 skewers.

1 skewer: 48 Calories; 2.3 g Total Fat (0.9 g Mono, 0.2 g Poly, 0.9 g Sat); 18 mg Cholesterol; 4 g Carbohydrate; 1 g Fibre; 3 g Protein; 50 mg Sodium

Sticks & Skewers

Greek Potato Skin Skewers

Greek-inspired flavours top satisfying skewered potato skins—serve these on the patio to kick-start a barbecue!

Medium unpeeled baking potatoes	3	3
Bamboo skewers (8 inches, 20 cm, each), soaked in water for 10 minutes	12	12
Olive (or cooking) oil	2 tbsp.	30 mL
Lemon pepper	1 tsp.	5 mL
Dried oregano	1/2 tsp.	2 mL
Garlic powder	1/2 tsp.	2 mL
Crumbled feta cheese	1 cup	250 mL
Finely chopped red onion	2 tbsp.	30 mL
Finely chopped black olives	1 tbsp.	15 mL
Chopped fresh parsley (or 1/4 tsp., 1 mL, flakes)	2 tsp.	10 mL

Wrap each potato in foil. Bake on centre rack in 425°F (220°C) oven for about 1 1/2 hours until tender. Transfer to cutting board. Carefully remove foil. Let stand until cool enough to handle. Cut potatoes lengthwise into quarters. Scoop out pulp, leaving 1/4 inch (6 mm) shell. Reserve pulp for another use. Thread shells lengthwise onto skewers.

Combine next 4 ingredients in small cup. Brush over both sides of shells. Arrange skewers, skin-side up, on ungreased baking sheet with sides. Bake for about 10 minutes until starting to brown. Turn.

Combine remaining 4 ingredients in small bowl. Scatter over shells. Bake for about 7 minutes until cheese is softened. Makes 12 skewers.

1 skewer: 64 Calories; 5.1 g Total Fat (2.4 g Mono, 0.3 g Poly, 2.2 g Sat); 11 mg Cholesterol; 3 g Carbohydrate; trace Fibre; 2 g Protein; 172 mg Sodium

Raspberry Basil Scallops

Scallop skewers make a light yet satisfying appetizer before heavier barbecue fare. Try garnishing with raspberries and basil leaves to give your guests a hint of the sweet and savoury flavours they are about to enjoy.

Chopped red onion	3 tbsp.	45 mL
Raspberry vinegar	3 tbsp.	45 mL
Olive (or cooking) oil	2 tbsp.	30 mL
Chopped fresh basil	1 tbsp.	15 mL
(or 3/4 tsp., 4 mL, dried)		
Granulated sugar	1 tbsp.	15 mL
Water	1 tbsp.	15 mL
Salt	1/8 tsp.	0.5 mL
Coarsely ground pepper	1/2 tsp.	2 mL
Small bay scallops	36	36
Bamboo skewers (4 inches, 10 cm, each), soaked in water for 10 minutes	12	12

Process first 8 ingredients in blender or food processor until smooth.

Place scallops in small shallow dish. Pour onion mixture over top. Marinate, covered, in refrigerator, stirring occasionally, for 1 hour.

Thread scallops onto skewers. Discard any remaining marinade. Arrange skewers on greased baking sheet with sides. Broil on centre rack in oven for about 4 minutes until scallops are opaque. Makes 12 skewers.

1 skewer: 27 Calories; 1.1 g Total Fat (0.7 g Mono, 0.1 g Poly, 0.2 g Sat); 6 mg Cholesterol; 1 g Carbohydrate; trace Fibre; 3 g Protein; 39 mg Sodium

Moroccan Pork Bites

These elegant and exotic nibbles of pork and juicy apple are glazed with sweet and spicy flavours.

Cooking oil	1/4 cup	60 mL
Liquid honey	3 tbsp.	45 mL
Lemon juice	1 tbsp.	15 mL
Chili powder	1/2 tsp.	2 mL
Ground cinnamon	1/2 tsp.	2 mL
Ground coriander	1/2 tsp.	2 mL
Ground cumin	1/2 tsp.	2 mL
Salt	1/2 tsp.	2 mL
Turmeric	1/2 tsp.	2 mL
Pork tenderloin, trimmed of fat, cut into 16 pieces	3/4 lb.	340 g
Unpeeled medium tart apples (such as Granny Smith), cut into 8 wedges each	2	2
Bamboo skewers (4 inches, 10 cm, each), soaked in water for 10 minutes	16	16

Combine first 9 ingredients in medium bowl. Reserve 1 tbsp. (15 mL) in small cup.

Add pork to cooking oil mixture in medium bowl. Stir until coated. Marinate, covered, in refrigerator for 30 minutes. Remove pork. Discard any remaining marinade.

Cut apple wedges in half crosswise. Thread apple and pork onto skewers. Arrange on greased wire rack set in foil-lined baking sheet with sides. Broil on top rack in oven for about 4 minutes per side until pork is no longer pink inside. Brush with reserved cooking oil mixture. Makes 16 bites.

1 bite: 61 Calories; 2.9 g Total Fat (1.6 g Mono, 0.7 g Poly, 0.4 g Sat); 14 mg Cholesterol; 4 g Carbohydrate; trace Fibre; 5 g Protein; 55 mg Sodium

Falafel with Curry Yogurt

Tiny falafel balls to dip in creamy curry yogurt—these are sure to be a star attraction at any party! Reheat on an ungreased baking sheet in a 400°F (200°C) oven for about eight minutes until crisp and heated through.

CURRY YOGURT

Plain yogurt	1/2 cup	125 mL
Mayonnaise	1 tbsp.	15 mL
Curry powder	1 tsp.	5 mL
Liquid honey	1/2 tsp.	2 mL
Salt, just a pinch		
Pepper, just a pinch		

FALAFEL

Can of chickpeas (garbanzo beans), rinsed and drained	19 oz.	540 mL
Large egg	1	1
Tahini (sesame paste)	1 tbsp.	15 mL
Ground coriander	1 tsp.	5 mL
Ground cumin	1 tsp.	5 mL
Garlic cloves, minced (or 1/2 tsp., 2 mL, powder)	2	2
Salt	1/2 tsp.	2 mL
Pepper	1/2 tsp.	2 mL
Dried crushed chilies	1/4 tsp.	1 mL
Chopped fresh chives (or green onion)	2 tbsp.	30 mL
Fine dry bread crumbs	2 tbsp.	30 mL
Chopped fresh cilantro (or parsley)	1 tbsp.	15 mL
Cooking oil	3 cups	750 mL
Cocktail picks	30	30

Curry Yogurt: Combine all 6 ingredients in small bowl. Chill, covered, for 30 minutes to blend flavours. Makes about 1/2 cup (125 mL).

Falafel: Process chickpeas in food processor with on/off motion until finely chopped. Add next 8 ingredients. Process until smooth. Transfer to medium bowl.

(continued on next page)

Add next 3 ingredients. Mix well. Form into 30 balls, using about 1 tbsp. (15 mL) for each.

Heat cooking oil in Dutch oven on medium-high until bread cube turns brown in 1 minute (350° to 375°F, 175° to 190°C). Shallow-fry balls, in 2 batches, for about 2 minutes until golden brown. Transfer with slotted spoon to paper towel-lined plate to drain. Insert cocktail picks into balls. Makes 30 falafel. Serve with Curry Yogurt.

1 falafel with 3/4 tsp. (4 mL) yogurt: 45 Calories; 3.0 g Total Fat (1.3 g Mono, 0.8 g Poly, 0.3 g Sat); 7 mg Cholesterol; 3 g Carbohydrate; 1 g Fibre; 1 g Protein; 70 mg Sodium

Pictured on page 36 and on back cover.

Antipasto Skewers

Big, bold flavours in a petite party skewer—classic Italian antipasto platter meets portable convenience in these delectable morsels with a savoury herb vinaigrette.

Olive oil	1/2 cup	125 mL
Balsamic vinegar	2 tbsp.	30 mL
White wine vinegar	2 tbsp.	30 mL
Italian seasoning	1 tsp.	5 mL
Salt	1/4 tsp.	1 mL
Pepper	1 tsp.	5 mL
Small fresh whole white mushrooms	12	12
Grape tomatoes	12	12
Pitted whole black olives	12	12
Bamboo skewers (6 inches, 15 cm, each)	12	12
Genoa salami slices, folded into quarters	12	12
Provolone cheese cubes (3/4 inch, 2 cm, pieces)	12	12

Combine first 6 ingredients in medium bowl.

Add next 3 ingredients. Stir until coated. Marinate, covered, in refrigerator for 6 hours or overnight, stirring occasionally. Drain, reserving olive oil mixture.

Thread vegetables onto skewers with salami and cheese. Brush with reserved olive oil mixture. Makes 12 skewers.

1 skewer: 175 Calories; 16.2 g Total Fat (9.9 g Mono, 1.3 g Poly, 4.6 g Sat); 18 mg Cholesterol; 2 g Carbohydrate; trace Fibre; 6 g Protein; 358 mg Sodium

Lox and Bagel Skewers

A deconstructed favourite with an appetizing look—smoked salmon and lemony cream cheese top soft bagel bites.

Block cream cheese, softened	8 oz.	250 g
Chopped fresh dill (or 3/4 tsp., 4 mL, dried)	1 tbsp.	15 mL
Finely chopped capers (optional)	2 tsp.	10 mL
Grated lemon zest	1/2 tsp.	2 mL
Smoked salmon slices, cut into thirty-two 3/4 inch (2 cm) strips	4 oz.	113 g
Cooking oil	1 tbsp.	15 mL
Bagels, split	2	2
Sprigs of fresh dill, for garnish		
Cocktail picks	32	32

Combine first 4 ingredients in small bowl. Chill, covered, for about 2 hours until firm. Roll into 3/4 inch (2 cm) balls.

Wrap smoked salmon strips around cheese balls.

Brush cooking oil over cut sides of bagels. Arrange on baking sheet. Broil on top rack in oven for about 1 minute until golden. Cut each half into 8 pieces. Place cheese balls on bagel pieces.

Garnish with dill sprigs. Secure with cocktail picks. Makes 32 skewers.

1 skewer: 57 Calories; 3.3 g Total Fat (1.1 g Mono, 0.3 g Poly, 1.7 g Sat); 9 mg Cholesterol; 5 g Carbohydrate; trace Fibre; 2 g Protein; 98 mg Sodium

Pictured at right.

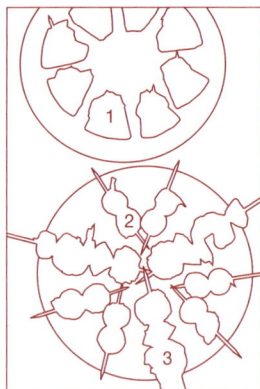

1. Lox and Bagel Skewers, above
2. Marinated Bocconcini Bites, page 127
3. California Sushi Skewers, page 114

124 Sticks & Skewers

Marinated Bocconcini Bites

Simple and colourful with complex flavours. Mild bocconcini cheese,
marinated in a sweet and tangy balsamic blend, is paired with grape
tomatoes and basil to create one-bite delights.

Balsamic vinegar	1/2 cup	125 mL
Sun-dried tomatoes in oil, blotted dry, finely chopped	1/4 cup	60 mL
Granulated sugar	2 tsp.	10 mL
Dried crushed chilies	1/2 tsp.	2 mL
Garlic clove, minced (or 1/4 tsp., 1 mL, powder)	1	1
Salt	1/4 tsp.	1 mL
Cocktail bocconcini (fresh mozzarella)	18	18
Grape tomatoes	18	18
Fresh basil leaves	18	18
Cocktail picks	18	18

Combine first 6 ingredients in small bowl. Transfer to medium resealable freezer bag. Add bocconcini. Seal bag. Turn until coated. Marinate in refrigerator for at least 6 hours or overnight, turning occasionally. Remove bocconcini. Discard any remaining marinade.

Thread tomatoes, basil leaves and bocconcini onto cocktail picks. Makes 18 bites.

1 bite: 26 Calories; 1.9 g Total Fat (trace Mono, trace Poly, 0.6 g Sat); 3 mg Cholesterol; 1 g Carbohydrate; trace Fibre; 2 g Protein; 24 mg Sodium

Pictured on page 125.

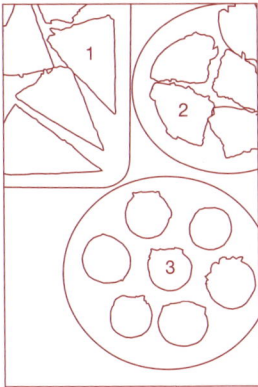

1. Tortilla Pizza Wedges, page 136
2. Smoked Salmon Waffle Bites, page 139
3. Spicy Chicken-stuffed Mushrooms, page 138
Props: Ikea

Coconut Chicken Waves

Chili-speckled chicken skewers with savoury lime and garlic—delicious served with a small dish of Thai peanut sauce for dipping.

Coconut milk	1 cup	250 mL
Brown sugar, packed	2 tbsp.	30 mL
Lime juice	2 tbsp.	30 mL
Dried crushed chilies	1 tsp.	5 mL
Salt	3/4 tsp.	4 mL
Garlic clove, minced	1	1
(or 1/4 tsp., 1 mL, powder)		
Boneless, skinless chicken breast halves	4	4
(4 – 6 oz., 113 – 170 g, each),		
cut lengthwise into 4 strips each		
Bamboo skewers (8 inches, 20 cm, each),	16	16
soaked in water for 10 minutes		

Combine first 6 ingredients in medium shallow bowl. Add chicken. Stir until coated. Marinate, covered, in refrigerator for 4 to 6 hours, stirring occasionally.

Remove chicken. Thread onto skewers. Discard any remaining marinade. Preheat gas barbecue to medium. Arrange skewers on greased grill. Close lid. Cook for 6 to 8 minutes per side until chicken is no longer pink inside. Makes 16 skewers.

1 skewer: 45 Calories; 1.5 g Total Fat (0.1 g Mono, 0.1 g Poly, 1.1 g Sat); 16 mg Cholesterol; 1 g Carbohydrate; trace Fibre; 7 g Protein; 56 mg Sodium

Sesame Pork Skewers

Savoury pork skewers with bites of sweet shrimp—they're tasty on their own, but can also be paired with a dipping sauce.

Chopped fresh mint (or 1 1/2 tsp., 7 mL, dried)	2 tbsp.	30 mL
Fine dry bread crumbs	2 tbsp.	30 mL
Lime juice	2 tsp.	10 mL
Soy sauce	2 tsp.	10 mL
Finely grated ginger root (or 1/4 tsp., 1 mL, ground ginger)	1 tsp.	5 mL
Pepper	1/2 tsp.	2 mL
Garlic clove, minced (or 1/4 tsp., 1 mL, powder)	1	1
Lean ground pork	1/2 lb.	225 g
Uncooked shrimp (peeled and deveined), chopped	1/4 lb.	113 g
Bamboo skewers (6 inches, 15 cm, each), soaked in water for 10 minutes	12	12
Sesame oil (for flavour)	2 tbsp.	30 mL

Combine first 7 ingredients in medium bowl.

Add pork and shrimp. Mix well. Divide into 12 equal portions. Form each portion into a 3 inch (7.5 cm) long log.

Thread logs onto ends of skewers. Arrange in an alternating pattern on greased wire rack set on baking sheet with sides (see Note). Brush with sesame oil. Broil on centre rack in oven for about 9 minutes until no longer pink inside. Makes 12 skewers.

1 skewer: 86 Calories; 6.6 g Total Fat (1.8 g Mono, 0.4 g Poly, 1.9 g Sat); 28 mg Cholesterol;
1 g Carbohydrate; trace Fibre; 5 g Protein; 107 mg Sodium

Note: Arranging the skewers with the stick ends on alternating sides of the baking sheet will insulate the skewers and reduce scorching.

Bourbon Chicken Bites

Enjoy the flavour of popular Buffalo chicken wings without the sticky fingers! These fiery chicken bites have a bold blue cheese sauce that can also be served with crisp vegetable sticks.

Bourbon whiskey	1/4 cup	60 mL
Chili powder	1 tsp.	5 mL
Dried oregano	1 tsp.	5 mL
Pepper	1/8 tsp.	0.5 mL
Boneless, skinless chicken thighs, cut into twenty-seven 1 inch (2.5 cm) pieces	1 lb.	454 g
Louisiana hot sauce	2 tbsp.	30 mL
Butter (or hard margarine), melted	2 tsp.	10 mL
Ranch dressing	1/4 cup	60 mL
Crumbled blue cheese	2 tbsp.	30 mL
Cocktail picks	27	27

Combine first 4 ingredients in small bowl. Put chicken into large resealable freezer bag. Pour whiskey mixture over top. Seal bag. Turn until coated. Marinate in refrigerator for 6 hours or overnight, turning occasionally. Remove chicken. Discard any remaining marinade. Arrange in single layer on greased baking sheet with sides. Cook in 450°F (230°C) oven for about 10 minutes until no longer pink inside.

Combine hot sauce and butter in large bowl. Add chicken. Stir until coated. Arrange on serving platter.

Whisk dressing and cheese in small bowl until combined. Insert cocktail picks into chicken. Serve with dressing mixture. Makes 27 chicken bites.

1 chicken bite with 1/2 tsp. (2 mL) dressing mixture: 42 Calories; 2.8 g Total Fat (0.6 g Mono, 0.3 g Poly, 0.8 g Sat); 13 mg Cholesterol; trace Carbohydrate; trace Fibre; 3 g Protein; 70 mg Sodium

Pictured on page 36 and on back cover.

Rosemary Onion Brie

Soft brie is served with a sweet-and-sour mixture of caramelized onions and balsamic, infused with the inviting aroma of rosemary. Serve with crackers, toasted baguette slices or buttered toast cut into triangles.

Thinly sliced onion	2 cups	500 mL
Balsamic vinegar	1/4 cup	60 mL
Butter	1 tbsp.	15 mL
Sprig of fresh rosemary	1	1
Salt	1/8 tsp	0.5 mL
Pepper, just a pinch		
Granulated sugar	1/2 tsp.	2 mL
Brie cheese round	4 oz.	125 g

Combine first 6 ingredients in large frying pan. Bring to a boil. Reduce heat to medium. Cook, covered, for about 5 minutes, stirring occasionally, until onion is softened.

Add sugar. Heat and stir for about 3 minutes until sugar is dissolved and liquid is almost evaporated.

Spoon over cheese round. Serve immediately. Serves 6.

1 serving: 103 Calories; 7.2 g Total Fat (2.0 g Mono, 0.2 g Poly, 4.5 g Sat); 24 mg Cholesterol; 6 g Carbohydrate; 1 g Fibre; 4 g Protein; 185 mg Sodium

Ginger Shrimp Canapés

Ginger marmalade adds just the right touch to a warmly spiced shrimp mixture and crisp Melba toasts. Crackers also work well for these canapés.

Mayonnaise	2 tbsp.	30 mL
Ginger marmalade	1 tbsp.	15 mL
Mild curry paste	1 tsp.	5 mL
Grated lime zest	1/4 tsp.	1 mL
Chopped cooked shrimp (peeled and deveined)	2/3 cup	150 mL
Round Melba toasts	16	16
Coarsely ground pepper, for garnish		

Combine first 4 ingredients in small bowl.

Add shrimp. Stir. Spoon onto Melba toasts.

Sprinkle with pepper. Makes 16 canapés.

1 canapé: 34 Calories; 1.5 g Total Fat (trace Mono, 0.1 g Poly, 0.2 g Sat); 13 mg Cholesterol; 3 g Carbohydrate; trace Fibre; 2 g Protein; 59 mg Sodium

Spicy Peanut Dip

Sambal oelek adds spice to this smooth, pleasing dip with a peanutty punch. This goes well with any vegetables you have on hand, but is especially nice with snap peas, carrots and peppers. Serve it with cooked shrimp for an extra-special treat.

Peanut butter	1/2 cup	125 mL
Plain yogurt	1/2 cup	125 mL
Lemon juice	2 tbsp.	30 mL
Chili paste (sambal oelek)	1 tbsp.	15 mL
Soy sauce	1 tbsp.	15 mL
Sesame (or cooking) oil	1 tsp.	5 mL
Garlic clove, chopped (or 1/4 tsp., 1 mL, powder)	1	1
Finely chopped green onion	1 tbsp.	15 mL

(continued on next page)

Process first 7 ingredients in blender until smooth. Transfer to serving bowl. Add green onion. Stir. Makes about 1 1/4 cups (300 mL).

1/4 cup (60 mL): 173 Calories; 13.8 g Total Fat (6.1 g Mono, 3.6 g Poly, 2.7 g Sat); 1 mg Cholesterol; 8 g Carbohydrate; 2 g Fibre; 8 g Protein; 460 mg Sodium

---

Beef Satay Skewers

Ginger marmalade is the secret ingredient in the peanutty glaze. Thick steaks are best for the thin slices needed for threading—preheat the broiler and soak the skewers while slicing the meat and you've got appies in no time!

Peanut butter	1/2 cup	125 mL
Hot water	3 tbsp.	45 mL
Cooking oil	1 tbsp.	15 mL
Ginger marmalade	1 tbsp.	15 mL
Lime juice	1 tbsp.	15 mL
Soy sauce	1 tbsp.	15 mL
Garlic clove, minced (or 1/4 tsp., 1 mL, powder)	1	1
Cayenne pepper	1/8 tsp.	0.5 mL
Beef top sirloin steak, trimmed of fat	1 lb.	454 g
Bamboo skewers (8 inches, 20 cm, each), soaked in water for 10 minutes	12	12
Salt, sprinkle		
Pepper, sprinkle		

Whisk first 8 ingredients in small bowl until combined.

Thinly slice steak across the grain (see Tip, page 112). Thread beef, accordion-style, onto skewers. Sprinkle with salt and pepper. Brush both sides with peanut butter mixture. Arrange on greased baking sheet with sides. Broil on top rack in oven for 2 minutes. Turn. Brush with remaining peanut butter mixture. Broil for about 2 minutes until starting to brown. Makes 12 skewers.

1 skewer: 159 Calories; 10.2 g Total Fat (4.7 g Mono, 2.0 g Poly, 2.6 g Sat); 28 mg Cholesterol; 4 g Carbohydrate; 1 g Fibre; 14 g Protein; 183 mg Sodium

Quick Red Pepper Guacamole

Roasted red peppers create cheery red bits in this quick and simple guacamole. It's smooth and fresh, just like it should be! Serve with tortilla chips.

Chopped avocado	3 cups	750 mL
Chopped roasted red peppers	1/4 cup	60 mL
Salsa	1/4 cup	60 mL
Lime juice	2 tbsp.	30 mL
Chopped fresh cilantro (or parsley)	1 tbsp.	15 mL
Salt	1/4 tsp.	1 mL
Pepper	1/8 tsp.	0.5 mL

Mash avocado with fork in medium bowl.

Add remaining 6 ingredients. Stir well. Makes about 3 1/4 cups (800 mL).

1/4 cup (60 mL): 62 Calories; 5.1 g Total Fat (3.4 g Mono, 0.6 g Poly, 0.7 g Sat); 0 mg Cholesterol; 4 g Carbohydrate; 2 g Fibre; 1 g Protein; 98 mg Sodium

Pictured on page 17.

Salmon Celery Boats

Smoked salmon creates a novel filling for celery sticks. The rich blend of salmon and cream cheese makes a simple and fun appetizer.

Block cream cheese, softened	1/4 cup	60 mL
Finely chopped smoked salmon	1/4 cup	60 mL
(about 1 1/4 oz., 35 g)		
Coarsely ground pepper	1/4 tsp.	1 mL
Grated lemon zest	1/4 tsp.	1 mL
Celery ribs, cut into 3 inch (7.5 cm) pieces	8	8
Chopped fresh chives (or finely chopped green onion)	2 tsp.	10 mL

Combine first 4 ingredients in small bowl. Spread into celery pieces.

Sprinkle with chives. Makes 24 boats.

1 boat: 12 Calories; 0.9 g Total Fat (0.3 g Mono, 0.1 g Poly, 0.6 g Sat); 3 mg Cholesterol; trace Carbohydrate; trace Fibre; 1 g Protein; 29 mg Sodium

Red Pepper and Peanut Hummus

Use roasted red peppers to whip up this vibrantly coloured hummus, which is made with peanut butter instead of the usual tahini (sesame seed paste).

Can of chickpeas (garbanzo beans), rinsed and drained	19 oz.	540 mL
Chopped roasted red peppers	1 cup	250 mL
Smooth peanut butter	1/2 cup	125 mL
Lemon juice	1/4 cup	60 mL
Olive (or cooking) oil	2 tbsp.	30 mL
Ground cumin	1 tsp.	5 mL
Garlic clove, chopped (or 1/4 tsp., 1 mL, powder)	1	1
Ground allspice	1/4 tsp.	1 mL
Salt	1/4 tsp.	1 mL

Process all 9 ingredients in food processor until smooth. Makes about 3 cups (750 mL).

1/4 cup (60 mL): 142 Calories; 8.4 g Total Fat (4.5 g Mono, 2.0 g Poly, 1.4 g Sat); 0 mg Cholesterol; 12 g Carbohydrate; 3 g Fibre; 5 g Protein; 288 mg Sodium

Spiced Ginger Cheese Spread

Keep ginger marmalade and sambal oelek handy to make this quick spread. It's sweet and tangy with a punch of curry heat—perfect to serve with crackers, pita, toast or muffins. Try it on celery sticks with raisins on top!

Block cream cheese, softened	8 oz.	250 g
Ginger marmalade	2 tbsp.	30 mL
Chili paste (sambal oelek)	1 tsp.	5 mL
Ground ginger	1/2 tsp.	2 mL
Mild curry paste	1/2 tsp.	2 mL
Salt	1/4 tsp.	1 mL

Beat all 6 ingredients in small bowl until smooth. Makes about 1 1/3 cups (325 mL).

2 tbsp. (30 mL): 83 Calories; 7.3 g Total Fat (2.1 g Mono, 0.3 g Poly, 4.6 g Sat); 23 mg Cholesterol; 3 g Carbohydrate; trace Fibre; 2 g Protein; 135 mg Sodium

Tortilla Pizza Wedges

Start with flour tortillas and basil pesto, and you've got tempting, pizza-like wedges in under half an hour.

Basil pesto	3 tbsp.	45 mL
Flour tortillas (9 inch, 23 cm, diameter)	2	2
Sliced fresh white mushrooms	1/2 cup	125 mL
Chopped red pepper	1/4 cup	60 mL
Sliced green onion	2 tbsp.	30 mL
Grated Italian cheese blend	1 cup	250 mL

Spread pesto over tortillas, almost to edge. Place, pesto-side up, on greased baking sheet.

Scatter next 3 ingredients over pesto.

Sprinkle with cheese. Bake in 450°F (230°C) oven for about 8 minutes until cheese is melted and tortillas are golden. Let stand on pan for 1 minute. Cuts into 10 wedges each for a total of 20 wedges.

1 wedge: 43 Calories; 2.1 g Total Fat (0 g Mono, 0 g Poly, 0.5 g Sat); 2 mg Cholesterol; 4 g Carbohydrate; trace Fibre; 2 g Protein; 109 mg Sodium

Pictured on page 126.

Sweet Pea Dip

Basil pesto combines with green peas to create the perfect dip for any occasion. This dip is particularly suited to summer entertaining when you've got garden-fresh peas. If you haven't got any white kidney beans on hand, chickpeas work just as well.

Frozen tiny peas	2 cups	500 mL
Water	1 tbsp.	15 mL
Can of white kidney beans, rinsed and drained	19 oz.	540 mL
Basil pesto	4 tsp.	20 mL
Lemon juice	1 tbsp.	15 mL
Olive (or cooking) oil	1 tbsp.	15 mL

(continued on next page)

Combine peas and water in medium microwave-safe bowl. Microwave, covered, on high for about 2 minutes until tender (see Tip, page 11). Drain. Rinse with cold water. Drain well. Transfer to food processor.

Add remaining 4 ingredients. Process until smooth. Makes about 2 1/3 cups (575 mL).

1/4 cup (60 mL): 97 Calories; 3.2 g Total Fat (1.1 g Mono, 0.1 g Poly, 0.4 g Sat); 1 mg Cholesterol; 13 g Carbohydrate; 4 g Fibre; 5 g Protein; 88 mg Sodium

Strawberry Brie Canapés

Creamy brie pairs with pretty strawberries to create these striking canapés. Slice the brie when cold for the neatest slices, or use a knife dipped in hot water.

Red wine vinegar	3 tbsp.	45 mL
Granulated sugar	1 tbsp.	15 mL
Medium fresh strawberries, quartered	6	6
Brie cheese round	4 oz.	125 g
Baguette bread slices, about 1/2 inch (12 mm) each	12	12
Coarsely ground pepper, for garnish		

Combine vinegar and sugar in small bowl. Add strawberries. Stir until coated. Let stand, covered, for 15 minutes.

Cut cheese round into twelve 1/4 inch (6 mm) slices. Place cheese slices on bread slices. Arrange on greased baking sheet with sides. Bake in 425°F (220°C) oven for about 5 minutes until cheese is softened. Drain and discard vinegar mixture from strawberries. Arrange strawberries over cheese.

Sprinkle with pepper. Makes 12 canapés.

1 canapé: 63 Calories; 3.0 g Total Fat (0.8 g Mono, 0.1 g Poly, 1.7 g Sat); 10 mg Cholesterol; 6 g Carbohydrate; trace Fibre; 3 g Protein; 117 mg Sodium

Pictured on page 144.

Dill Pickle Ham Rolls

Flour tortillas roll up to create creamy spirals with the yummy flavour combination of pickles and ham. You can use whatever tortillas you have on hand for these, although whole-wheat or cheese-flavoured ones are particularly nice.

Chopped fresh spinach (or lettuce) leaves, lightly packed	3/4 cup	175 mL
Block cream cheese, softened	4 oz.	125 g
Finely chopped dill pickle	1/3 cup	75 mL
Dijon mustard	2 tbsp.	30 mL
Flour tortillas (9 inch, 23 cm, diameter)	3	3
Shaved deli ham	6 oz.	170 g

Combine first 4 ingredients in small bowl.

Spread over tortillas, leaving 1/2 inch (12 mm) edge.

Arrange ham in single layer over cheese mixture. Roll up tightly, jelly-roll style. Trim ends. Cut each roll diagonally into 8 pieces. Makes 24 rolls.

1 roll: 48 Calories; 2.5 g Total Fat (0.5 g Mono, 0.1 g Poly, 1.2 g Sat); 8 mg Cholesterol; 4 g Carbohydrate; trace Fibre; 2 g Protein; 211 mg Sodium

Spicy Chicken-stuffed Mushrooms

Sambal oelek creates the "spicy" in these cute stuffed mushrooms packed with chicken and green onion. Impressive results from a last-minute appetizer!

Chopped cooked chicken (see Tip, page 140)	3/4 cup	175 mL
Mayonnaise	1 tbsp.	15 mL
Sliced green onion	1 tbsp.	15 mL
Chili paste (sambal oelek)	1 tsp.	5 mL
Pepper, sprinkle		
Medium fresh whole white mushrooms, stems removed	12	12
Cooking spray		

(continued on next page)

Last-minute Bites

Combine first 5 ingredients in small bowl.

Spray mushrooms with cooking spray. Arrange in single layer on baking sheet with sides. Fill with chicken mixture. Bake in 425°F (220°C) oven for about 10 minutes until mushrooms are tender and filling is heated through. Makes 12 stuffed mushrooms.

1 stuffed mushroom: 30 Calories; 1.6 g Total Fat (0.2 g Mono, 0.2 g Poly, 0.3 g Sat); 8 mg Cholesterol; 1 g Carbohydrate; 0 g Fibre; 3 g Protein; 23 mg Sodium

Pictured on page 126.

Smoked Salmon Waffle Bites

Smoked salmon tops these delicious and entirely unexpected appetizers. Just pull some waffles out of the freezer—these bites are best with buttermilk or whole-wheat varieties. If you don't have any frozen waffles, you can also use crackers or toast.

Sour cream	1/2 cup	125 mL
Chopped English cucumber (with peel)	1/4 cup	60 mL
Chopped seeded tomato	1/4 cup	60 mL
Salt	1/8 tsp.	0.5 mL
Coarsely ground pepper	1/2 tsp.	2 mL
Frozen waffles, toasted	3	3
Smoked salmon slices (about 4 oz., 113 g), halved	6	6
Red onion slivers, for garnish	12	12

Combine first 5 ingredients in small bowl.

Cut waffles into quarters. Spoon sour cream mixture onto waffle pieces.

Top with salmon. Garnish with onion. Makes 12 bites.

1 bite: 60 Calories; 2.8 g Total Fat (0.2 g Mono, 0.1 g Poly, 1.5 g Sat); 11 mg Cholesterol; 5 g Carbohydrate; trace Fibre; 3 g Protein; 157 mg Sodium

Pictured on page 126.

Chicken Pesto Quesadillas

With flour tortillas, basil pesto and a few simple grocery items, you can whip together these flavourful quesadilla wedges—full of cheesy goodness and sure to please a crowd!

Chopped cooked chicken (see Tip, below)	1/2 cup	125 mL
Chopped seeded tomato	1/4 cup	60 mL
Basil pesto	1 tbsp.	15 mL
Grated Italian cheese blend	1/2 cup	125 mL
Flour tortillas (9 inch, 23 cm, diameter)	2	2
Cooking oil	1 tsp.	5 mL

Combine first 3 ingredients in small bowl.

Sprinkle 2 tbsp. (30 mL) cheese over half of each tortilla. Spoon chicken mixture over cheese. Sprinkle remaining cheese over top. Fold tortillas in half to cover filling. Press down lightly.

Heat cooking oil in large frying pan on medium. Add quesadillas. Cook for about 4 minutes until bottom is golden. Turn. Cook for about 1 minute until bottom is golden and cheese is melted. Cuts into 4 wedges each for a total of 8 wedges.

1 wedge: 94 Calories; 4.1 g Total Fat (0.6 g Mono, 0.3 g Poly, 1.0 g Sat); 10 mg Cholesterol; 8 g Carbohydrate; trace Fibre; 6 g Protein; 194 mg Sodium

tip Don't have any leftover chicken? Start with 2 boneless, skinless chicken breast halves (4 – 6 oz., 113 – 117 g, each). Place in large frying pan with 1 cup (250 mL) water or chicken broth. Simmer, covered, for 12 to 14 minutes until no longer pink inside. Drain. Chop. Makes about 2 cups (500 mL) of cooked chicken.

Mocha Pots de Crème

What's not to love? Petite pots of dark chocolate and coffee custard provide a not-too-sweet ending to a meal or appetizer menu—each pot delightfully topped with a chocolate-covered coffee bean.

Half-and-half cream	1 1/4 cup	300 mL
Granulated sugar	2 tbsp.	30 mL
Instant coffee granules, crushed to fine powder	1 tbsp.	15 mL
Egg yolks (large)	3	3
Dark chocolate bars (3 1/2 oz., 100 g, each), chopped	3	3
Vanilla extract	1/2 tsp.	2 mL
Chocolate-covered coffee beans, for garnish	6	6

Combine first 3 ingredients in medium saucepan. Heat and stir on medium for about 5 minutes until sugar is dissolved and mixture is hot, but not boiling.

Whisk egg yolks in small bowl until smooth and light. Whisk in 2 tbsp. (30 mL) cream mixture. Slowly add egg mixture to cream mixture in saucepan, whisking constantly. Cook on medium for 1 minute, stirring constantly. Remove from heat.

Add chocolate and vanilla. Stir until chocolate is melted. Strain though fine sieve into medium bowl. Pour into 6 small ramekins or small cups. Cool. Chill, covered, for 6 hours or overnight.

Garnish with coffee beans. Serves 6.

1 serving: 380 Calories; 24.6 g Total Fat (2.6 g Mono, 0.6 g Poly, 14.9 g Sat); 124 mg Cholesterol; 36 g Carbohydrate; 5 g Fibre; 5 g Protein; 38 mg Sodium

Pictured on page 143.

Raspberry Rosé Granita

Deliciously vibrant flavour to match the gorgeous colour. This refreshing treat makes a great dessert for a patio party—just serve in small sherry glasses or shooters. This will store in a tightly sealed container in the freezer for up to three months.

Granulated sugar	1 cup	250 mL
Water	3/4 cup	175 mL
Fresh (or frozen, thawed) raspberries	3 cups	750 mL
White zinfandel (or rosé) wine	1 1/2 cups	375 mL
Lemon juice	3 tbsp.	45 mL

Fresh raspberries, for garnish

Combine sugar and water in small saucepan. Bring to a boil, stirring constantly. Reduce heat to medium. Boil gently, uncovered, for 1 minute. Remove from heat. Cool completely.

Process next 3 ingredients in blender or food processor until smooth. Strain through fine sieve into medium bowl, pressing mixture through sieve with back of spoon. Discard solids. Add sugar mixture. Stir. Pour into 2 quart (2 L) baking dish. Freeze, covered, for 6 hours or overnight until firm. Scrape with spoon to break up ice crystals. Spoon into small glasses or bowls.

Garnish with raspberries. Makes about 7 cups (1.75 L).

1/4 cup (60 mL): 33 Calories; 0 g Total Fat (0 g Mono, 0 g Poly, 0 g Sat); 0 mg Cholesterol; 7 g Carbohydrate; trace Fibre; trace Protein; 1 mg Sodium

Pictured at right.

1. Raspberry Rosé Granita, above
2. Mocha Pots de Crème, page 141

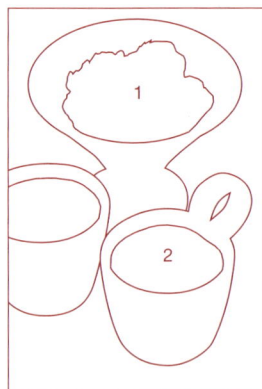

Small Sweets

Chocolate Hazelnut Tarts

Cute tarts with a simple, tasty filling of chocolate hazelnut spread and a light whipped cream topping.

Frozen mini tart shells, thawed	18	18
Chocolate hazelnut spread	1/3 cup	75 mL
Whipping cream	1/2 cup	125 mL
Hazelnut liqueur	1 tbsp.	15 mL
Icing (confectioner's) sugar	2 tsp.	10 mL
Chocolate curls, for garnish (see Note)		

Arrange tart shells on ungreased baking sheet with sides. Bake in 375°F (190°C) oven for about 12 minutes until golden. Cool.

Spread hazelnut spread evenly in bottom of each tart shell.

Beat remaining 3 ingredients in small bowl until soft peaks form. Makes about 1 cup (250 mL). Spoon over hazelnut spread.

Garnish with chocolate curls. Makes 18 tarts.

1 tart: 128 Calories; 8.3 g Total Fat (1.2 g Mono, 0.3 g Poly, 3.8 g Sat); 13 mg Cholesterol; 12 g Carbohydrate; trace Fibre; 1 g Protein; 74 mg Sodium

Note: To make chocolate curls, scrape chocolate firmly along its length with a swivel vegetable peeler.

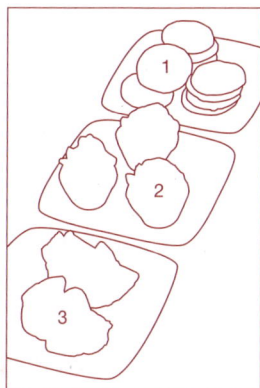

1. Tomato Basil Shortbread, page 33
2. Orange Poppy Seed Cupcakes, page 146
3. Strawberry Brie Canapés, page 137

Orange Poppy Seed Cupcakes

Sweet and lovely treats for the grown-ups, these cute mini-cupcakes have crunchy poppy seeds and a buttery-smooth icing spiked with orange liqueur.

All-purpose flour	3/4 cup	175 mL
Brown sugar, packed	1/3 cup	75 mL
Poppy seeds	1 tbsp.	15 mL
Baking powder	1 tsp.	5 mL
Baking soda	1/4 tsp.	1 mL
Salt	1/8 tsp.	0.5 mL
Butter (or hard margarine), softened	1/4 cup	60 mL
Large egg	1	1
Buttermilk (or soured milk, see Tip, right)	1/3 cup	75 mL
Orange juice	2 tbsp.	30 mL
Grated orange zest (see Tip, page 93)	1 tsp.	5 mL
ORANGE FROSTING		
Icing (confectioner's) sugar	1 cup	250 mL
Butter (or hard margarine), softened	1/4 cup	60 mL
Orange liqueur	1 tbsp.	15 mL

Combine first 6 ingredients in medium bowl. Add butter. Beat on low until mixture is crumbly.

Combine next 4 ingredients in small bowl. Add to butter mixture. Beat on high until smooth. Fill 18 paper-lined mini-muffin cups full. Bake in 350°F (175°C) oven for about 12 minutes until wooden pick inserted in centre of cupcake comes out clean. Let stand in pan for 10 minutes before removing to wire racks to cool completely.

Orange Frosting: Beat all 3 ingredients on low in small bowl until smooth. Beat on high for about 3 minutes until light and fluffy. Makes about 2/3 cup (150 mL). Spoon into piping bag fitted with large star tip (see Tip, page 43). Pipe onto cupcakes. Makes 18 mini-cupcakes.

1 mini-cupcake: 114 Calories; 5.6 g Total Fat (1.5 g Mono, 0.4 g Poly, 3.4 g Sat); 25 mg Cholesterol; 15 g Carbohydrate; trace Fibre; 1 g Protein; 108 mg Sodium

Pictured on page 144.

Cranberry Biscotti Bites

People will love the novel concept of these two-bite biscotti—perfect for enjoying with tea, coffee or wine. They're pleasantly sweet and packed with chocolate, cranberries and rich walnuts. As an added perk, this sweet treat freezes particularly well.

Butter (or hard margarine), softened	1/4 cup	60 mL
Granulated sugar	1/2 cup	125 mL
Large egg	1	1
Cranberry cocktail	2 tbsp.	30 mL
Vanilla extract	1/2 tsp.	2 mL
All-purpose flour	1 1/2 cups	375 mL
Chopped walnuts	1/4 cup	60 mL
Dried cranberries	1/4 cup	60 mL
Mini semi-sweet chocolate chips	1/4 cup	60 mL
Baking powder	3/4 tsp.	4 mL
Salt	1/4 tsp.	1 mL

Beat butter and sugar in medium bowl until light and creamy. Add egg. Beat well.

Add cranberry cocktail and vanilla. Beat until combined.

Combine remaining 6 ingredients in small bowl. Add to butter mixture. Mix until stiff dough forms. Turn out onto lightly floured surface. Knead 6 times. Divide into 2 portions. Shape into 12 inch (30 cm) long logs. Place on greased baking sheet. Flatten slightly. Bake in 350°F (175°C) oven for about 18 minutes until edges are golden. Let stand on baking sheet for about 10 minutes until cool enough to handle. Using serrated knife, cut logs diagonally into 1/2 inch (12 mm) slices. Arrange on ungreased baking sheet. Bake in 275°F (140°C) oven for about 15 minutes until bottoms are golden. Turn slices over. Turn oven off. Let stand in oven for about 30 minutes until dry and crisp. Makes about 42 biscotti.

1 biscotti: 46 Calories; 2.1 g Total Fat (0.5 g Mono, 0.4 g Poly, 1.0 g Sat); 8 mg Cholesterol; 7 g Carbohydrate; 2 g Fibre; 1 g Protein; 33 mg Sodium

tip To make soured milk, measure 1 tbsp. (15 mL) white vinegar or lemon juice into a 1 cup (250 mL) liquid measure. Add enough milk to make 1 cup (250 mL). Stir. Let stand for 1 minute.

Caramelized Apple Samosas

These sugar-dusted phyllo pastries have a buttery filling of sweet apple and crunchy poppy seeds—tempting treats akin to apple turnovers.

Chopped peeled cooking apple (such as McIntosh)	3 cups	750 mL
Lemon juice	1 tbsp.	15 mL
Butter (or hard margarine)	1 tbsp.	15 mL
Brown sugar, packed	3 tbsp.	45 mL
Vanilla extract	1/2 tsp.	2 mL
Ground cinnamon	1/4 tsp.	1 mL
Ground almonds	2 tbsp.	30 mL
Poppy seeds	1 tbsp.	15 mL
Phyllo pastry sheets, thawed according to package directions	6	6
Butter (or hard margarine), melted	1/4 cup	60 mL
Icing (confectioner's) sugar, for garnish		

Toss apple and lemon juice in medium bowl.

Melt first amount of butter in large frying pan on medium. Add apple mixture. Cook for about 10 minutes, stirring often, until apple is tender-crisp.

Add next 3 ingredients. Cook for about 5 minutes, stirring occasionally, until apple is tender.

Add almonds and poppy seeds. Stir.

Place 1 pastry sheet on work surface. Cover remaining sheets with damp towel to prevent drying. Brush sheet with second amount of butter. Cut lengthwise into 4 strips. Spoon about 1 tbsp. (15 mL) apple mixture onto bottom of strip. Fold 1 corner diagonally towards straight edge to form triangle. Continue folding back and forth, to enclose filling (see diagram). Repeat with remaining pastry sheets, butter, and remaining apple mixture. Arrange on greased baking sheets with sides (see Note). Brush with remaining butter. Bake in 375°F (190°C) oven for about 15 minutes until golden. Let stand on baking sheet for 5 minutes.

Sprinkle with icing sugar. Makes 24 samosas.

(continued on next page)

Small Sweets

1 samosa: 54 Calories; 3.1 g Total Fat (1.0 g Mono, 0.3 g Poly, 1.6 g Sat); 6 mg Cholesterol; 6 g Carbohydrate; 1 g Fibre; 1 g Protein; 40 mg Sodium

Pictured on page 108.

Note: Samosas can be frozen uncooked at this point. Brush frozen samosas with butter. Bake in 375°F (190°C) oven for about 18 to 20 minutes until golden and heated through.

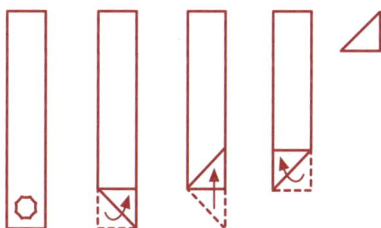

Chocolate Orange Mousse

Enjoy the perfectly paired flavours of orange and dark chocolate in this smooth, light mousse. Serve in espresso cups or small ramekins and garnish with fresh berries or orange segments.

Dark chocolate bar, chopped	3 1/2 oz.	100 g
Ricotta cheese	2 cups	500 mL
Milk	1/2 cup	125 mL
Granulated sugar	1 tbsp.	15 mL
Grated orange zest	1/2 tsp.	2 mL
Vanilla extract	1/2 tsp.	2 mL

Put chocolate into small microwave-safe bowl. Microwave on medium for about 60 seconds, stirring every 30 seconds, until almost melted (see Tip, page 11). Stir until smooth.

Process remaining 5 ingredients in blender or food processor until combined. With motor running, slowly add chocolate through hole in lid or feed chute until smooth. Spoon into 8 small cups or bowls. Chill for 4 hours. Serves 8.

1 serving: 179 Calories; 11.2 g Total Fat (0.1 g Mono, 0 g Poly, 7.2 g Sat); 27 mg Cholesterol; 9 g Carbohydrate; 1 g Fibre; 9 g Protein; 108 mg Sodium

Baklava Bundles

Appealing bundles with a delectably sweet filling peeking out—the nuts, seeds and honey are chewy and delicious with a great toasted flavour.

Chopped walnuts, toasted (see Tip, page 77)	1/4 cup	60 mL
Finely chopped pistachios, toasted (see Tip, page 77)	1/4 cup	60 mL
Granulated sugar	2 tbsp.	30 mL
Roasted sesame seeds	2 tbsp.	30 mL
Ground cinnamon	1/4 tsp.	1 mL
Liquid honey	3 tbsp.	45 mL
Butter (or hard margarine), melted	2 tbsp.	30 mL
Lemon juice	2 tsp.	10 mL
Vanilla extract	1/2 tsp.	2 mL
Package of puff pastry (14 oz., 397 g), thawed according to package directions	1/2	1/2

Combine first 5 ingredients in medium bowl.

Whisk next 4 ingredients in small bowl. Add 3 tbsp. (45 mL) to walnut mixture. Stir.

Roll out puff pastry on lightly floured surface to 12 inch (30 cm) square. Cut into quarters. Cut each quarter into 4 squares for a total of 16 squares. Spoon about 1 1/2 tsp. (7 mL) walnut mixture onto centre of 1 pastry square. Fold bottom corner over filling. Fold side corners over filling. Roll up toward top corner. Pinch seam against roll to seal. Arrange, seam-side down, on parchment paper-lined baking sheet with sides. Repeat with remaining walnut mixture and pastry squares. Brush bundles with remaining honey mixture. Using sharp knife, cut small slash across top of each bundle. Bake in 375°F (190°C) oven for about 20 minutes until pastry is puffed and golden. Let stand on baking sheet for 5 minutes before removing to wire rack to cool. Makes 16 bundles.

1 bundle: 111 Calories; 7.5 g Total Fat (1.0 g Mono, 1.2 g Poly, 2.1 g Sat); 4 mg Cholesterol; 10 g Carbohydrate; 1 g Fibre; 2 g Protein; 79 mg Sodium

Pictured on page 108.

Raspberry Hazelnut Brownies

These raspberry-topped chocolate brownies come complete with a delightfully creamy icing, and are filled with toasted hazelnut flavour.

Semi-sweet chocolate baking squares (1 oz., 28 g, each), chopped	2	2
Granulated sugar	1 1/2 cups	375 mL
All-purpose flour	2/3 cup	150 mL
Cocoa, sifted if lumpy	1/2 cup	125 mL
Flaked hazelnuts (filberts), toasted (see Tip, page 77)	1/2 cup	125 mL
Salt	1/4 tsp.	1 mL
Large eggs	3	3
Cooking oil	1/3 cup	75 mL
Vanilla extract	1 tsp.	5 mL
Mascarpone cheese	1/2 cup	125 mL
Icing (confectioner's) sugar	3 tbsp.	45 mL
Flaked hazelnuts (filberts), toasted	2 tbsp.	30 mL
Fresh (or frozen, thawed) raspberries	36	36

Put chocolate into small microwave-safe bowl. Microwave, uncovered, on medium for about 90 seconds, stirring every 30 seconds, until almost melted (see Tip, page 11). Stir until smooth.

Combine next 5 ingredients in medium bowl. Make a well in centre.

Whisk next 3 ingredients in small bowl. Add chocolate. Whisk until smooth. Add to well. Stir until just combined. Spread evenly in greased 9 x 9 inch (23 x 23 cm) pan. Bake in 350°F (175°C) oven for about 25 minutes until wooden pick inserted in centre comes out moist but not wet with batter. Do not overbake. Let stand in pan on wire rack until cool.

Beat mascarpone and icing sugar in small bowl until smooth. Spread over brownies.

Sprinkle with hazelnuts. Top with raspberries. Cuts into 36 squares.

1 square: 105 Calories; 7.2 g Total Fat (2.5 g Mono, 0.9 g Poly, 2.3 g Sat); 25 mg Cholesterol; 10 g Carbohydrate; 1 g Fibre; 2 g Protein; 26 mg Sodium

Pictured on page 108.

Measurement Tables

Throughout this book measurements are given in Conventional and Metric measure. To compensate for differences between the two measurements due to rounding, a full metric measure is not always used. The cup used is the standard 8 fluid ounce. Temperature is given in degrees Fahrenheit and Celsius. Baking pan measurements are in inches and centimetres as well as quarts and litres. An exact metric conversion is given below as well as the working equivalent (Metric Standard Measure).

Spoons

Conventional Measure	Metric Exact Conversion Millilitre (mL)	Metric Standard Measure Millilitre (mL)
1/8 teaspoon (tsp.)	0.6 mL	0.5 mL
1/4 teaspoon (tsp.)	1.2 mL	1 mL
1/2 teaspoon (tsp.)	2.4 mL	2 mL
1 teaspoon (tsp.)	4.7 mL	5 mL
2 teaspoons (tsp.)	9.4 mL	10 mL
1 tablespoon (tbsp.)	14.2 mL	15 mL

Cups

Conventional Measure	Metric Exact Conversion Millilitre (mL)	Metric Standard Measure Millilitre (mL)
1/4 cup (4 tbsp.)	56.8 mL	60 mL
1/3 cup (5 1/3 tbsp.)	75.6 mL	75 mL
1/2 cup (8 tbsp.)	113.7 mL	125 mL
2/3 cup (10 2/3 tbsp.)	151.2 mL	150 mL
3/4 cup (12 tbsp.)	170.5 mL	175 mL
1 cup (16 tbsp.)	227.3 mL	250 mL
4 1/2 cups	1022.9 mL	1000 mL (1 L)

Dry Measurements

Conventional Measure Ounces (oz.)	Metric Exact Conversion Grams (g)	Metric Standard Measure Grams (g)
1 oz.	28.3 g	28 g
2 oz.	56.7 g	57 g
3 oz.	85.0 g	85 g
4 oz.	113.4 g	125 g
5 oz.	141.7 g	140 g
6 oz.	170.1 g	170 g
7 oz.	198.4 g	200 g
8 oz.	226.8 g	250 g
16 oz.	453.6 g	500 g
32 oz.	907.2 g	1000 g (1 kg)

Oven Temperatures

Fahrenheit (°F)	Celsius (°C)
175°	80°
200°	95°
225°	110°
250°	120°
275°	140°
300°	150°
325°	160°
350°	175°
375°	190°
400°	200°
425°	220°
450°	230°
475°	240°
500°	260°

Pans

Conventional Inches	Metric Centimetres
8x8 inch	20x20 cm
9x9 inch	23x23 cm
9x13 inch	23x33 cm
10x15 inch	25x38 cm
11x17 inch	28x43 cm
8x2 inch round	20x5 cm
9x2 inch round	23x5 cm
10x4 1/2 inch tube	25x11 cm
8x4x3 inch loaf	20x10x7.5 cm
9x5x3 inch loaf	23x12.5x7.5 cm

Casseroles

CANADA & BRITAIN		UNITED STATES	
Standard Size Casserole	Exact Metric Measure	Standard Size Casserole	Exact Metric Measure
1 qt. (5 cups)	1.13 L	1 qt. (4 cups)	900 mL
1 1/2 qts. (7 1/2 cups)	1.69 L	1 1/2 qts. (6 cups)	1.35 L
2 qts. (10 cups)	2.25 L	2 qts. (8 cups)	1.8 L
2 1/2 qts. (12 1/2 cups)	2.81 L	2 1/2 qts. (10 cups)	2.25 L
3 qts. (15 cups)	3.38 L	3 qts. (12 cups)	2.7 L
4 qts. (20 cups)	4.5 L	4 qts. (16 cups)	3.6 L
5 qts. (25 cups)	5.63 L	5 qts. (20 cups)	4.5 L

Recipe Index

154

155

158

HEALTHY COOKING SERIES

To your health—and bon appétit!

You've asked and Company's Coming has listened! The new Healthy Cooking Series delivers delicious healthy recipes and nutrition information from leading health and wellness experts. These beautiful, full-colour cookbooks will transform the way you eat—and the way you live!

Now Available!

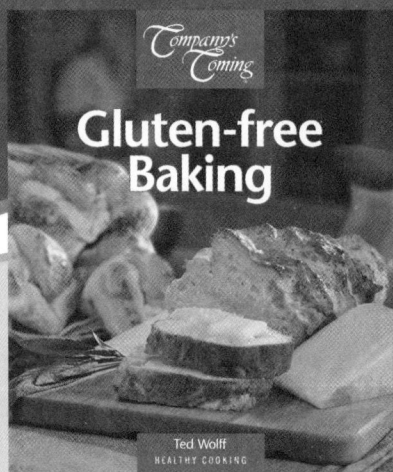

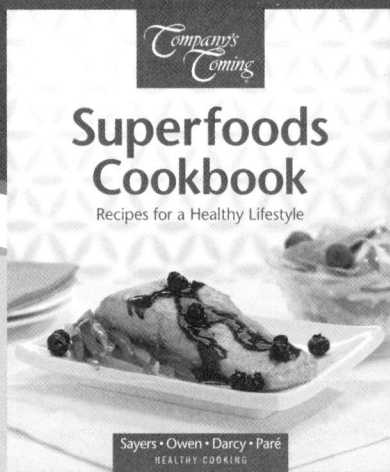

Company's Coming

Gluten-free Baking

Ted Wolff
HEALTHY COOKING

Finally—a book that shows you how to make delicious baked goods and sweets that are completely gluten-free. Ted Wolff, founder of Kinnikinnick Foods, makes living gluten-free easy in this highly requested title.

Now Available!

Company's Coming

Superfoods Cookbook

Recipes for a Healthy Lifestyle

Sayers • Owen • Darcy • Paré
HEALTHY COOKING

Blueberries lower your risk for cardiovascular disease, and walnuts reduce your risk of diabetes and cancer. With these recipes, you can easily add superfoods to your daily diet and improve your health and well-being.

Company's Coming

Get free recipes, preview new titles and sign up to receive our online newsletter:

www.companyscoming.com

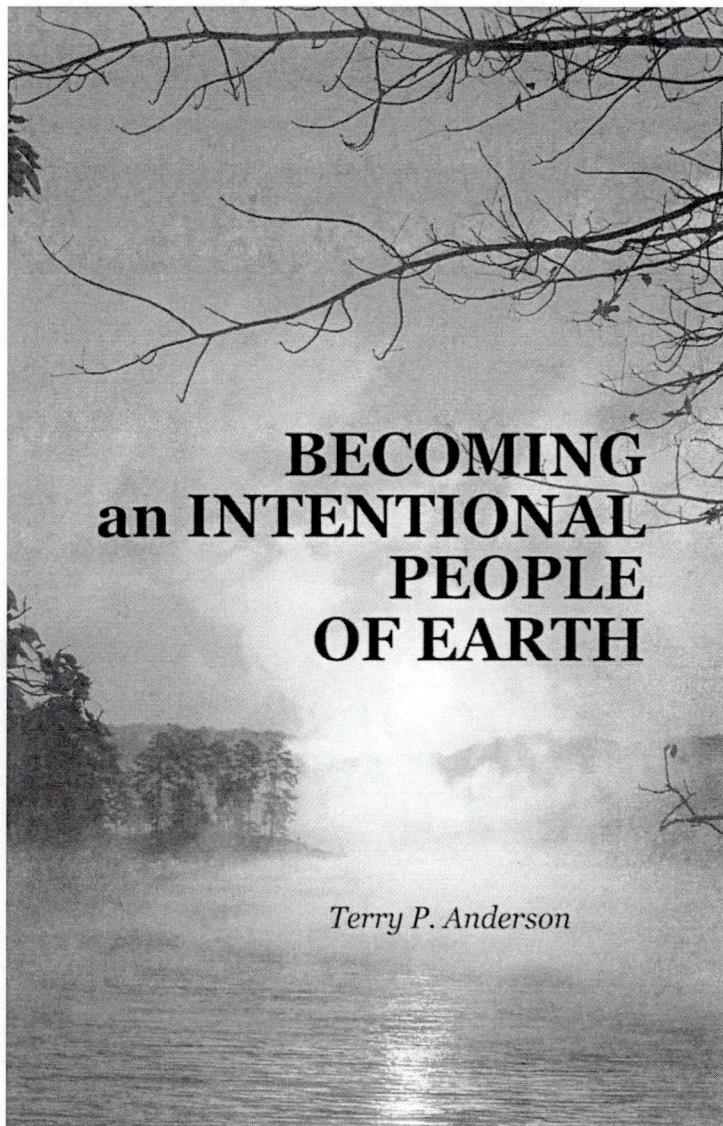

BECOMING
an INTENTIONAL
PEOPLE
OF EARTH

Terry P. Anderson

Becoming an Intentional People of Earth

PUBLISHER
Path of Potential
P.O. Box 4058, Grand Junction, CO 81502

AUTHOR
Terry P. Anderson

EDITOR
Sandra Maslow Smith

COVER PHOTO
Vernon G. Maslow

Second Edition, First Printing
2015
Printed in the United States of America

OTHER WRITINGS from PATH OF POTENTIAL

The Living Library of Potential: www.pathofpotential.org
Path of Potential on Facebook: www.facebook.com/pathofpotential

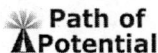

Path of
Potential is a trademark of TS Potential, LLC

ISBN-13: 978-0-9966909-0-4

BECOMING
an INTENTIONAL
PEOPLE
OF EARTH

Terry P. Anderson

Path of
Potential

Second Edition...
With expanded
Introductory and Closing Reflections

The now needed being shift...

The stirring, the intentional stirring, the intuitive awakening of heart and mind is strengthening. The need for a shift in being, along the path of our becoming, has an increasing sense of urgency – urging us towards embracing the whole of the truth of the Source...

The whole of the truth of the Source as lifted up by Pope Francis when he starts his thinking from the philosophical beliefs of Francis of Assisi...

The beliefs of all-inclusive love, and our being creatures of life – meant to honor and live harmoniously with our Sister, Mother Earth; not to have dominion over...

Beliefs requiring our shifting from a human centered perspective to a life of the whole centered perspective...

Beliefs also requiring the development of philosophy that – as Pope John Paul II called for – is whole enough and complete enough for people of all walks of life to come together in dialogue to resolve issues such as ecology, race and poverty; philosophy that enables the forming of thought and culture such that the genuine ethics so urgently needed today can be formulated...

A now needed being shift that moves us away from divisiveness and towards wholeness... wholeness and the truth of our oneness...

An authentic shift along the path of our becoming... becoming an intentional people of earth... a true people of life...

A shift that calls upon intuition, the intuition of wholeness, that which we look to when we seek to see, not from existence, but from essence – to see from above...

A shift that begins not from structure or hierarchy; but rather with process – the grassroots process of intentional dialoguing...

Terry P. Anderson

July 2015

CONTENTS

Forward

We are not the source of truth, love or good.
Through intuitive processing, intentional dialoguing and
prayerful questioning, we have gained access to some
images of intentionality which are the source of this
writing.

To be clear, if, in your reflective reading and
dialoguing of what is written here, you see or experience
a sense of truth, know for certain it does not come from
the writer.

Introduction

WITHIN THE HEART
OF THE PROCESS

Our Potential for Becoming Intentional

We are created in the image and likeness of God… a yet to be realized image and likeness… an unrealized potential that lies within – within our innermost self.

+ God is intentional… the way of God is intentional… intentional ways made visible through the living word and the living earth. *We have yet to be, yet to become intentional.*

+ The love of the Source is all-inclusive… inclusive of each and all. We are not the source of all-inclusive love; but have within, the potential to be vessels for the love of the Source entering into the working of the world… entering into our ways of being and doing. *We have yet to be and become vessels for all-inclusive love entering into the here and unfolding now.*

+ God is life… the Source of life – the whole of life, the living earth. We are of and from the life… not separate from life; but rather inextricably woven within the ways of life… the intended ways of working of life on this earth. *We have yet to join in… to be and become intentional instruments for the ongoing and upward unfolding of life… yet to join with the Creator, our Creator, in the eternalizing of life on and through the living earth.*

4

Now is the time of potential... a time for realizing the potential our Creator has endowed, intentionally endowed, within us... a time for making real the truth of our having been created in the image and likeness of our Creator... a time for intentional ways – for joining in the Father-Creator's work... a time for all-inclusive love entering... a time for embracing the wholeness of life – our livingness... a time for our being and becoming an authentic people of life – for our being and becoming an intentional people of earth.

5

The Reconciling Power of Work

At the center, at the heart of realizing our unrealized potential, is work – called work, intentional work, work of now... work that we come to and need to understand by and through the works and the word:

> By reflecting on the works, the working of the creation, the working of ourselves, culture, etc. - seeing intended ways of working of life.

> And by reflecting on the word – seeing the word from a life of the whole perspective.

Work is that which reconciles – encompasses all and makes whole - the truth of the works and the truth of the word; the word and the works come together in a yin/yang way through work.

The living philosophy of potential encompasses both word and works, and embraces the essence of each. All of which in a summary way is captured within "Becoming an Intentional People of Earth":

> Being an instrument for inspiriting life,

> Becoming a vessel for love – the all-inclusive love, the all-nourishing love of the Source – entering living earth.

Part 1

THE STIRRING TOWARDS BECOMING

There is a Stirring

Food for Dialogue...

There is, for more and more of us, a stirring... an inner stirring that is awakening within, the intuitive questioning and seeking... a seeking that is drawing us towards and into reflective processes... the necessary space for accessing intuition, particularly the intuition of wholeness... the intuitive processing required for ourselves, for our communities, to move towards wholeness and away from the pervasive fractionating, divisive processes that are actively present throughout our society, its institutions, and essential processes – educating, habitat-ing, family-ing, recreating, etc.... pervasive processes rich in anger and argument; but void of resolving power with regard to the issues now before us... and consequently lacking any real hope... real hope for the children, real hope for the whole of life on earth.

Emerging from these reflective spaces and processes – the dwelling place and working space of intuition – is a seeing of the truth of wholeness... an intuitive understanding of the intimate inseparability of the wholeness of the children with the wholeness of life... a seeing of the reality that an inspirited future for the children can only occur – be possible – within the flourishing, truly vital and viable living earth...

These peaceful and calming spaces where the inner work of intuition can be heard and honored – honored through reflective processing – are bringing forth a seeing and understanding of a way forward that is not the way of today;

but rather an intentional way... an intentional way of life, of this living earth, and our living and working in ways congruent with intent... a seeing and understanding of pursuits, and ways of taking up such pursuits that...

Move us towards wholeness and away from divisiveness,

Work for all children, all children in the world,

Bring our world – our ways of living and working – into congruent harmony with intent... the intent of the Source – the Source of all, the Source of the living earth.

...pursuits that, given the intuitively seeable way we work, require a philosophy that is whole enough, complete enough for the work of now... and a philosophy that is practice-able and experientially validate-able. Such a philosophy is the living philosophy of potential, the essence of which is:

Earth was created as a space for life to enter into the working of the whole of creation; eternalizing life on and through earth is the work of the Source.

Man was created for life.

Life was not created for man.

Man's presence on earth is not accidental, but rather intentional.

As such, man, like all of life, has work and role... particular work and role with regard to the ongoingness and upward unfolding of life... a systemic relatedness with intent, the intent

of the Source, through the taking up of our work... our work and role within the whole of life.

...Always remembering of course, that if love – the all-inclusive love of now – is not present in the process, love will not be present in the outcomes, in the outflowing of truth and spirit into the working of our world, into our ways of living and working. It is through all-inclusive love entering that it becomes possible for our moving in the direction of being and becoming an intentional people of earth.

www.pathofpotential.org
www.facebook.com/pathofpotential

10

Taking up this Path

Food for Dialogue...

Taking up this path... the path of our becoming... our becoming as intended... our becoming an intentional people of earth, requires of us a new seeing, a new understanding...

Requires the development of a new seeing and understanding that is currently not present in the world of our making; not present in our ways, our pursuits, our paths...

Requires a seeing and understanding that emerges from, and is organized by original intent... by our embracing of original intent – that which preceded us, preceded our "No," our ongoing "No" to intended ways... to the intent which is still present... still present, patiently, urgently awaiting our authentic "Yes."

To be clear, original intent is not the intent with which we are familiar...

> The intent that we currently express or pursue...

> The intent that comes to us through reasoned interpretation of the word or the works.

> No, not that, but rather...

Original intent is that which becomes seeable, accessible, livable through our embracing – our being open to – the whole of the truth of the Source – the Source of love, the Source of life... through our embracing the inseparability of love and

life... love and life being the wholistic expression of the truth of the Source... a wholistic expression of the truth of the Source present within, but unrealized in humanity...

A humanity that has yet to become a vessel for the all-inclusive love of the Source entering into the working of the world...

A humanity yet to become an instrument for the eternalizing of life on and through earth...

Yet to become a vessel and an instrument living out the truth that...

At essence we are all equal, and...

*Through intent we are living human beings –
members in the ongoingness of life...*

A presence, an intentional presence... a potential yet to be realized...

A presence and potential now being called for... called forth and to be manifested through our becoming an intentional people of earth...

All of which only becomes possible if and when we shift from a human centered perspective to a life of the whole centered perspective...

For ultimately, the perspective we hold, where we start our thinking from, determines the path we take...

12

Part 2

MAKING THE STEP CHANGE OF NOW:

LIVING AND WORKING FROM A LIFE OF THE WHOLE PERSPECTIVE

The essential virtue at this time of potential is wholeness... our moving towards wholeness.

Taking a life of the whole perspective begins the process of our moving towards wholeness... the process leading to our becoming an intentional people of earth.

The Most Significant Question of All

Food for Dialogue...

These writings come about because of the experience one of my companions had while traveling in Ireland. She, who has celiac disease, had a very pleasant and surprising experience with some of the gluten containing food and drink she consumed during our trip. The experience being the gluten containing food and drink she consumed in Ireland did not have the debilitating effects of similar food and drink consumed back home in the U.S. ... and since this was not a singular incident, but rather an unfolding pattern, some questioning naturally bubbled up... questions such as:

> What's different here?
> Is it the processing... the grain itself – the natural structure
> or a genetically modified one?
> Is it their way of farming, the soil, the weather?
> And so forth.

...questioning that through reflection brought forth another pattern of questioning... questions such as:

> What is at work here? ...perhaps something larger, more
> wholistic, more systemic?
> Is celiac disease a symptom of something larger with
> regard to the ways of life, the working of life... with
> regard to our ways of living and working?
> And so forth.

14

Further reflection brought to mind the processes and patterns of reason and intuition... the former taking up pursuits related to problems, problem solving... grounded in existence... seeking knowledge regarding structure, structuring, construction... seemingly, always an energizing process that we look to for matters of existence - the structuring matters of existence. A mind and process we often equate with being highly knowledgeable, skilled, and very able with regard to reasoning processes; for example, problem solving, a capacity for manipulating structures and structuring towards desired ends, and an astuteness when it comes to reasoning, reasoned interpretation... a demonstrated ableness we often refer to in terms of smartness, being smart, intelligence, etc... a capacity and capability highly valued in an existence-based, reason-led culture.

The latter, intuition, taking up pursuits related to potential, the realizing of potential... grounded in essence patterns of intent... seeking ableness with regard to seeing process... seeing process because potential, realizing potential, lies in process - virtue, essence-patterns-of-intent-sourced processes... a wholistic and systemic seeing with regard to that. This is the mind and process we call upon to bring wisdom into our processes... our processes of life, of work... and in particular, at this time, the wisdom of intent... the guiding wisdom and understanding critical to the work of now:

Creating a culture that works for all children, all children in the world.

15

Bringing the world of our making into congruence with the world of intent.

Reflecting on our current path, our patterns and processes, it is obvious, intuitively obvious, that we are not lacking smartness. Not lacking the ability to generate and bring forth a myriad of possible structures is not what is at work here. No, it is not a lack of smartness; but rather a lack of wholeness, systemicness, and completeness of thought. That is what is at work here... a lacking, a void, which requires intuition, the intuition of wholeness... and now at this time, requires intentional intuition... the intuition that embraces wholeness and intent... a wholeness and intent that fully encompasses process... the intuition that holds process within heart and mind, and seeks to honor and enable process... the processes of life; the process of our becoming fully, truly and wholly human... our being and becoming an intentional people of earth... the intuition called upon for seeing process and accessing the wisdom of intent... the wisdom necessary for making increasingly wise choices... wise choices with regard to the children; wise choices with regard to life - the whole of life, our ways of living and working... choices that move us in the direction of intentionality... in the direction of our being and becoming an intentional people of earth.

...Always remembering, of course, that *if love is not present in the process, love will not be present in the outcomes.* It is love, all-inclusive love, that makes the intentional – intentional ways – possible.

16

And finally, perhaps – no, not perhaps, but rather undoubtedly - the most significant question of all... the original question, the forever question: What will we put our faith in? Will it be the intentional processes of life? The intentional processes of love – of our becoming fully, truly and wholly human?... or perhaps something else, some other path?

Life is...

Food for Dialogue...

Life is an intentionally driven upward process, an intentionally
– beyond our wishes and desires – driven process. Life's ways
are wholistic, systemic and cyclical... a practical reality for all
of life's members.

Whereas, through the segmenting processes of reason, it is
possible to see and engage life's process in fragmented, non-
systemic, hierarchical and linear ways; the truth of life is
manifested in and through its intentional process, and its
wholistic, systemic and cyclical ways... a reality present within
our emerging understanding of the inadequacy of non-systemic
notions – segmented, segmenting slices of life's process –
notions such as predator/prey and food chain hierarchy when it
comes to understanding and enabling the vitality of oceanic life
systems... and other life systems as well. We are not the
source of life.

Truth is an ongoing prevailing process... an unfolding, ever
deepening, increasingly whole process... a process whereby
the truths of the previous are neither dismissed nor diminished;
but rather are enfolded within the unfolding; emerging as a
more whole, more complete manifestation of truth. We can see
this at work in the compassion of caring for being enfolded
within the compassion of caring about - the all-inclusive
compassion of equality. We are not the source of truth.
However, through reflective intuitive processing, truth can
become accessible and seeable for us.

www.pathofpotential.org
www.facebook.com/pathofpotential

18

We are of and from life, and like all members of life, we have work – real work – with regard to the ongoingness of life, the intentionally driven upward unfolding process of life. Our work is not to diminish the vitality, the viability, the potential, the ongoingness of life. Of that we can be certain. Equally clear is the requirement for the development and implementation of intentional ways, for our being and becoming intentional with regard to our processes - our intuitive and reasoning processes.

And so… truth exists. Truth is accessible and seeable. An upward forward path is possible. Remembering, of course, that at this time, community is the smallest whole.

19

Love is...

Food for Dialogue...

Love is the process that makes all things possible. Love is a process of and from the Source. We are not the source; we are not the source of life, nor are we the source of love. Whereas life is the ongoing manifestation of the unfolding intent of the Source, and the source of all purposes, all work; love is the process by and through which we advance our humanness. Love is the process through which we move towards wholeness – wholeness of people and life, wholeness of thought and approach. And love is the process through which we move towards intent – towards our being and becoming intentional. Love - the unconditioned, unconditional love of the Source - like the nourishing renewing spring rain, is non-discriminatory... falling equally upon all - equally upon all regardless of beliefs, regardless of ideologies. The all-inclusive love of the Source is ever-present; continuously seeking an open vessel – an unconditioned heart... a heart free of guilt, fear, pride, contempt, etc.... a heart free of that which is ultimately about self.

Love, truly loving the Source, is manifested through the opening of the heart to love entering... and the opening of the mind to seeing the truths love makes visible... the eternal truths, the critical truths of now... the seeking and understanding of which comes about through the reflective processes of intuition; and, at this time when community is the smallest whole, through intentional dialoguing. All of which

requires a life of the whole perspective. Loving the Source, serving the Source, is a heart and mind process calling for the creating within of an unconditioned heart, and the developing of the mind that sees process, wholeness and systemic relatedness… creating and developing not only within the one, but particularly within the community.

Love, coming from love, takes us beyond the limitations of goodness – beyond the feelings present in doing good, being good – to willfulness… to our coming from and enabling Thy Will being done. And love takes us beyond the compassion of caring for, to seeing and embracing the compassion of equality – the process of loving one another in all-inclusive ways… ways that reflect the absence of worldly hierarchy… ways that shine the light of love upon the truth of our shared humanity, and the oneness that is present in our – each and all – being of and from the one and the same Source. It is through the compassion of equality, our coming from that – holding that in heart and mind – that we move towards intentionality… towards living out and from the all-inclusive love Christ, through his work, makes possible.

It is through self-serving pursuits of power and control – power and control over earth, over life, over others – that we turn our backs to the Source… that we harden our hearts and become impervious to love entering. When love is absent, so too is truth… and inevitably, illusion and artificiality displace reality – displace the realness, the intent and the purpose of life, the realness of our life, of our ways.

21

Our being and becoming an intentional people of earth becomes possible through and only through love... a truth that calls upon our becoming instruments of, and vessels for love entering into the world – the here and unfolding now... a calling that makes necessary our detaching from contempt – from our being captured in heart and mind by contempt, a seemingly ever-present, readily accessible contempt. Whereas love lifts all – each and all – up; contempt is an exhausting, dehumanizing burden for all... a burdensome process that moves us away from wholeness, away from love, away from the Source... a burdensome process that moves us towards divisiveness, away from reconciling issues in advancing humanness ways, and inevitably taking us along a path of anger and hate. Our detaching being a necessary process, not only within self, but also within community, within ourselves as a people; and particularly at this time, a call for detaching from ideological contempt.

And so, if our aim is to love and serve the Source, to move towards being and becoming an intentional people – a Thy Will people of earth... if that is the path of our choice:

Heart and mind will be moving towards wholeness – embracing the wholeness of creation, the wholeness of life, the wholeness of humanity;

Love and truth will be increasingly present in our work and roles... a love and truth at work within intentional grandmothering – the initiating role of now;

An unfolding path of love will be emerging… an unfolding path of love, truth and faith – true faith… having faith in love, having faith in intent… putting our faith in that.

Intentional Ethics are...

Food for Dialogue...

Intentional ethics are the process by which we, as a people, are systemically woven within the ongoing processes of life... a systemicness – systemic working, systemic ways – with regard to the whole of life not possible within our current ways of separateness... within our current way of seeing and acting as if we exist outside of, separate from the whole of life... a degree of separation and independence that naturally carries over to the Source as well. Our being intentionally ethical enables a systemic joining with the intentional ways and working of life that moves us towards becoming fully human... moving us away from our segmented ways, and towards living from the truth of our being intentionally created as living human beings, as a people of and from life; and like all creatures and systems of life, our having work and role, purposes and aims, with regard to the ongoingness of life... a reflection of the truth that ultimately "It is all about life"; and yet it is through love – the love of and from the Source – that all things become possible.

Intentional ethics move us beyond the limitations of the existence-based notions of legality and rights to the right and good... right for the one, good for the whole – the whole of humanity... right for humanity, good for the whole of life. And intentional ethics move us towards essence, our coming from essence... towards the truth that earth was not created for man; rather man – living man – was created for earth. As such

the land, the sea, the air, the water, belong not to us; but rather to the Source and to the intentional ways and unfolding of life. Ours is not to diminish the presence and processes of intent – intended ways, intended unfolding. No... that is neither our privilege nor our purpose; rather we are intended, and now called, to join in – to systemically join in – through taking up ways of working and living that enhance and inspirit life – the whole of life, ourselves included, but not only ourselves.

Intentional ethics are the process through which we ongoingly say "Yes" to the Father-Creator's command of eternal life – the eternalizing of life on and through earth... a process of saying "Yes" to life, the Source of life, the whole of life... a yes reflecting our livingness, our systemic work and role with regard to the ongoingness of life...

A yes not so much from obedience, an act of obedience, or acting from instinct; but rather an exercising of free will – a willful yes to intent, to the Source, to an intentional path. A yes free of non-wholistic cultural and ideological restraints, free to consciously choose the right and good... a path and process of consciously choosing – a choice of and from wholeness... of and from seeing wholeness, seeing process and systemic working. A free will, conscious choice process made possible through two or more gathering in reflective processing... made possible through reflective processing and our developing heart and mind for the work before us, the work for all children in the world – developing our ways, culture for that; and for our moving towards congruence with intent – bringing the world of our making into congruence with the world of intent.

25

It is the way of living systems to serve the larger whole... maintaining its integrity and intentionality, and sustaining the potential of the processes within. Our joining in, systemically joining in the ways of living systems, requires a seeing and understanding of wholeness and process... focusing on and starting from that. Seeing love and life in the light of this understanding has brought forth some imagery, some added seeing... a seeing of life as the heart, at the core of all purposes, all work – the heart and core of our purposes, our work. And seeing love as the life blood of our humanness... of the oneness and the wholeness of humanity – our shared humanity... seeing the life blood flowing through – unhindered, not conditionally interrupted or deflected – and nourishing each and all... nourishing every cell of the whole, bringing life to life... flowing through and penetrating deeply within the very fiber of our being, our human beingness... seeing love flowing through the unconditioned heart – the heart of the one, the heart of humanity... flowing through both in the returning sense – loving the Source – and in the becoming sense – loving one another. And through the life blood, the blood of life, we see our being and becoming intentional... our being and becoming a living vessel for love entering and flowing through; and our being and becoming a living systemic instrument for the ongoing eternalizing of life.

Whereas our being intentionally ethical, organizes – brings into being, makes real for us – the truth of our livingness, the process for our joining the Source of life, and our participation in the whole of life; intentional ethics are themselves organized – made practice-able – by the working of philosophy... a

particular philosophy organized around intent and work... a living philosophy of and from life... a developing philosophy that takes us beyond the limitations of our existence orientation and existence ways, to realizing our potential. A living philosophy of potential that takes us beyond the limitations of segmentation, segmented ways, and towards wholeness – wholeness of truth... the truths of our returning, the truths of our becoming... the truths of our livingness, the truths of our humanness... the truth of love, the truth of life. And thus is enabling of our living from the compassion of equality, and our pursuing congruence with intent.

Life and love... the unfolding of life, the ever flowing unchanging love, the life blood, the blood of life, emerge from the Will Force – the common Source of intent. It is when we take up living system ways – within humanity, within the whole of life – that it becomes possible for us to move towards becoming fully and truly human... possible for us to take up the path of original intent... to move towards realizing our potential to live from the truth of life, the truth of love... to move towards becoming fully human, a living instrument for the intended unfolding of life; and becoming truly human, a living vessel for love – the love that makes all things possible – entering and flowing into the world. For ultimately, it is our living in systemic ways – within ourselves as a people of earth, within the whole of life – that moves us towards wholeness... towards our becoming wholly – fully and truly human... moves us towards becoming an intentional – as intended – people of earth.

27

The Why of Essence

Food for Dialogue...

There is a force... a will force... a creative force... an intentionality... an intentional process, an essence pattern of intent, that permeates – is present within – the whole of life, and within ourselves as living human beings. It is through the enabling and manifesting of essence that our will becomes a manifestation of, congruent with, the will of the Source – the Source of love, the Source of life. It is in and through essence that the uniqueness of the one, and the oneness of Source – the common Source of all – become a manifestation, not of separateness, but rather of wholeness. At essence, we, each and all, are equal in potential – equal in the here and unfolding now potential - to participate in the intended unfolding... equal in potential to be and become a vessel for love entering, an instrument for the ongoingness of life.

It is through work and role, through our seeing and understanding of intended work and role, that essence becomes visible; innerly visible within the intentional ways of life... seeable, understandable and manifestable within our ways of living and working. It is essence that brings love and life systemically together... a systemic forming through which they – essence patterns of intent, love and life – become a systemic manifestation of the whole of the Source... the wholistic working of the Source... the whole of the truth of the Source. Essence is a process phenomenon – not a fixed structure; but rather an intentional pattern that is realized through process...

www.pathofpotential.org
www.facebook.com/pathofpotential

through beingness. We are not the source of essence, but rather enablers of.

It is essence that we turn to, look to, develop ableness with regard to; if we... if we and our ways – our ways of living and working – are to move towards congruence with intent... with the will of the Source. It is essence that we seek and embrace to have our ways of living and working be a reflection of, and means for, the will of the Source being done on this earth. It is through the seeing, and understanding of essence that we move beyond the limitations of reasoning, the limitations of reasoned interpretation... beyond the limitations of thingness, of doingness... beyond these towards being... towards being and beingness. It is through being, beingness, that we advance our humanness. Being is a process phenomenon, a product of interaction, a presence of wholeness that creates within an inner experience of oneness, of being at one... a systemic oneness with and within the whole. And, at this time of potential, a presence of particular wholeness – wholeness of life, wholeness of truth, wholeness of love.

At essence, the truth of the word is love – love in the process. At essence the truth of the works is life – the ongoing eternalizing of life. There is a pattern, a cyclical pattern of intent present within the way of truth. A pattern of increasing depth and wholeness – all-encompassing wholeness. A pattern of the truths of the previous being enfolded into the intended unfolding; emerging as deeper more wholistic expressions of the previous. A pattern present within the upward unfolding of life, the advancing of our humanness – our moving towards

becoming fully and truly human... present within our becoming an intentional people of earth. A pattern, a way of moving beyond existing limitations, that is also present within love and life. A pattern visible in the upward shift from love of the particular – the instinctive love of one's own family, tribe, etc. – to the all-inclusive love of the Source, the all-inclusive love of the Source brought to life – made accessibly present – through the work of Christ. A pattern present within the shift from the compassion of caring for to the compassion of equality – the love that acknowledges the equality of all: one Source; all else equal. We see this pattern in life as we shift from human centeredness to a life of the whole perspective. And too, we can see this pattern at work as we seek to organize – bring discipline and order to – our ways of working and living. Here we can see work ethic – the virtues of discipline, responsibility and dedication – being enfolded within intentional ways... intentional working, ethical ways... our living and working within the ways of intentional ethics.

There is a path... the oldest path, the original path... a virginal path... a path not of our making... a path of which we have little, if any, real – truthfully real – experience... a path yet to be taken... a path of intent, a path of original intent, a here and unfolding now path of potential... a forever, dynamic, inspiriting path of life. A path of essence, of enfolding and unfolding essential truths... the truths of the word, the truths of the works; the truth of love, the truth of life. There is a way... a way of love, a way of truth, a way of life... a way of encompassing wholeness and inclusivity. A way requiring the seeing of essence, requiring our moving towards wholeness,

and the developing of systemic and wholistic understanding...
the nature of seeing and understanding that comes to us
through process... the seeing of process that comes to us
through reflective intuitive processing. There is a way, a path
of potential – a path of and for realizing our potential... a
potential realization necessary for the eternalizing of life on
and through the earth... the realization of our potential to
become fully and truly human. A way of our being significant
and systemically relevant to the ongoing upward unfolding of
life... our enabling and enhancing the process of life; rather
than our being a diminisher of life's vitality and viability. A
way requiring our taking up of intentional ways... a way
requiring our taking on intended work and roles.

The truth of our work lies in essence... essence patterns of
intent... our "pollinating, soil making" work lies in essence, in
the enabling of and manifesting of essence... lies within the
manifesting of spirit... the inspiriting of life through work –
intended work and intentional ways. A work for all children in
the world culture is a culture of work... a culture of intentional
work, of working intentionally... a culture of intentional ethics.

31

Moving towards Wholeness... Taking up Intentional Pursuits

Food for Dialogue...

The word we commonly give to how humans organize to carry out work and generate value is business. A way of organizing that is not unlike the hiving of bees. As our business moves towards intentionality, being a truly human endeavor, it enfolds and unfolds in value adding – run up – ways... run up versus run down ways... run up with regard to the life processes of earth... run up in advancing humanness ways... run up in congruence with intent, intended ways. An enfolding and unfolding of truths, of essence ways; regardless of our business – be it material structuring, food growing, scientific discovering, entertaining, educating, governing, informing, etc.... and regardless of our field of endeavor – be it health care, service, sports, transporting, not for profit or for profit, etc. All of which are guided by intentional ethics and share a common core of being a virtue sourced, essence based, value adding process.

The essential virtue at this time of potential is wholeness – moving towards wholeness... wholeness of truth of the Source, wholeness of life, wholeness of humanity... wholeness of approach. A wholeness of approach that calls for developing the seeing mind of wisdom and for intentionalizing the knowing mind of reason... for embracing the wholeness of intent. A wholeness of approach which calls upon the process mind of intuition – the intuition of wholeness – and the

3

structuring mind of reason working in complementary, systemic, intentional ways... working wholistically... wholistically forming the process mind of intentionality – the mind of our being and becoming an intentional people of life... an authentic people of and from the Source. A process mind and a way of processing and dialoguing that reflects the reality that, at this time of potential, community is the smallest whole.

It is through work, intended work and role; through our virtue sourced, value adding work and intentional ways of working, that the intentional mind and the unconditioned heart become a systemic manifestation of the whole of humanity, the whole of the truth of humanity. A wholeness and systemicness present within and required for our being and becoming fully and truly human... our becoming an intentional people of life; an intentional, truly human – love in the process – people of earth... the living earth.

Part 3

WHERE TO BEGIN?

The now necessity for:

THE ROLE OF INTENTIONAL GRANDMOTHERING –

> *Becoming a vessel for the all-inclusive love of the Source entering into the working of the world by...*
>
> *Creating the active, living presence of a work for all children in the world culture;*

THE WORK OF ADVANCING OUR HUMANNESS –

> *Becoming an instrument for the intended eternalizing of life on and through earth by...*
>
> *Creating the active, working presence of intentional ethics...*
>
> *Bringing the world of our making into congruence with the world of intent.*

www.pathofpotential.org
www.facebook.com/pathofpotential

34

The Role of
Intentional Grandmothering
Becoming a Vessel for the All-inclusive Love of the
Source entering into the Working of the World

On a quiet contemplative evening, a woman, a grandmother to many, reflects on a question from her son... Did she, during her long life, experience any surprises? He watched in silence as she sifted backwardly through her life and as she reflectively formed a response... No... No surprises... Oh, yes, there was one surprise... I have been surprised as to how fast life has gone by. Her son then asked... How about regrets - any regrets? Again a period of silence... more reflective processing, a thoughtful, more considered response... No, not really... No real regrets. A response that brought an end to the questioning and an apparent shift, a deliberate shift, to the shared inner processing that was taking place... a shift in focus... moving away from herself, away from her life... and towards the children... not just her children's children, but all the children. Before her voice entered the silence, he could see in her eyes, in the expression on her face, that what she was about to say was deeply held. She spoke in a familiar, but infrequently used tone... a tone reserved for the serious, the serious truth, the truthfulness of what she was saying... she was saying, I worry about the children... a worry that emanated from what her heart and mind saw within our current ways and current culture. All of which – the look in her eyes, the expression on her face, the words she spoke, and the tone that

enshrouded them – created within her son a depth of feeling that is still readily accessible, ever deepening, today.

And now, through the seeing, imaging and understanding brought forth through intentional dialoguing, the necessity for intentional grandmothering has come to the fore... has been made clear... intentional grandmothering being a role, an initiating role, a process role... not a person, not a position, not a job. A role organized, not by expertise, but rather by intentional wisdom. The role required for taking up the work of creating the active, living presence of a work for all children in the world culture... the necessary work now before us; for it is culture - our ways, our culture - that ultimately determines who we are, why we are, and who we ourselves and our children will become.

And thus the mother's worry about the children, a worry shared by many, can be acted upon... responded to in advancing humanness ways. Through intentional presence, the beingness of the role of intentional grandmothering, the necessary process of moving towards wholeness, away from that which divides – the intended unfolding of now - can and is commencing...

An intentional presence that evokes willful attention to purpose, the intentional purpose of our and life's processes, systems and structures... willful attention to that which works for all children.

An intentional presence that brings conscience and wholistic understanding to the truth of our living nature... the truth, the inseparable reality, that a culture that works

for all children in the world understands that the vitality of life, of the living processes of earth and the ongoing wellbeing of the children are one and the same... the oneness of Source, a oneness with the Source, the Source of life... a oneness of people, a people of and from life. A work for all children culture is a culture that is free of the illusion that the diminishment of the vitality of the life processes and systems of earth is both necessary and justified with regard to sustaining our life and to the pursuit of our happiness.

An intentional presence, a seeing and sharing of wholistic understanding... a clarity, a conviction with regard to the world of intent... a world of wisdom, a world of wisdom and beauty... a flourishing, nourishing, living world.

Yes, intentional grandmothering will lead - will lead through process - and reason will follow... reason will become intentionally and purposefully employed. The beingness of the grandmothering role, through the intuition of wholeness - accessing, seeing and understanding the working of intentional wisdom - will lead. Leading will unfold from and through process – particularly engaging in processes of intentional reading, intentional writing, intentional dialoguing and prayerful questioning... processes that open the heart to the mother's command of *Work for all my children, all the children in the world...* processes that develop the mind – the wholistic seeing and understanding required – for creating the active presence of a work for all children in the world culture. And, yes, intentional wisdom will begin to guide reason...

www.pathofpotential.org
www.facebook.com/pathofpotential

guiding in ways such that what is brought forth into existence is increasingly congruent with intent... intended ways of working of life on this earth. Always remembering, of course, that *if love is not present in the process, love will not be present in the outcomes...* and it is the unconditioned love - the essence of the Source - that makes all things possible.

www.pathofpotential.org
www.facebook.com/pathofpotential

38

The Work of
Advancing our Humanness
Becoming an Instrument for the Intended
Eternalizing of Life on and through Earth

Technology - technological man - can cause a particular future: but, in and of itself, cannot create the future - the intended unfolding, the realizing of our human potential, the eternalizing of life on this earth... an eternalizing of life in the here and unfolding now that calls for honoring and enabling the nourishing, life giving capacity of the life systems and processes of this earth... that which is critical to our ongoing living, and critical to all of life.

We, as living human beings, can join in the intended unfolding; we, through work and role, can fully participate... a participation and joining in that requires a wholistic seeing and understanding of intended ways of working and the intentional, purposeful employment of reason in pursuits that are increasingly harmonious and congruent with intent... the intended ways of working of our life, the whole of life on this earth. All of which enables, makes possible, our moving in the direction of bringing the world of our making into congruence with the world of intent... a world of wisdom... a world of wisdom and beauty.

Our world, the world of our making, is increasingly a product of science factism... a reductionist process that diminishes our beingness, diminishes our humanness, and disconnects us from life - from the intended, the totally interconnected, ways of

working of life on this earth. All of which serves to move us away from, rather than towards, advancing our humanness. As beingness diminishes we naturally move towards increasingly coarser and coarser energies, seeking more and more artificial stimulations… which in turn habitually capture our attention, time and resources. Science factism, like other ideologies, has within it a level of attractiveness, a certain drawing power to particular concepts and ideals; but, as is common to ideologies, lacks wholeness, the necessary wholeness and completeness required for the work before us, and as such is not a real path, not a path of and towards congruence with intent.

Bringing the world of our making into congruence with the world of intent both requires and is initiated by the active, working presence of ethics – more specifically, intentional ethics. Congruence with intent, if it is to become practice-able – made real – will require the active working presence of intentional ethics, that which is right for humanity, good for the whole of life… that which enables a coalescing, a moving towards wholeness of conscience and heart – that which we innerly know to be right and good.

Creating the active, working presence of intentional ethics is complementary to, the kindred spirit of, creating the active presence of a work for all children in the world culture… a kindred spiritness that requires both a living philosophy that is whole enough and complete enough for the work before us, and a shift in starting perspective – shifting from human centered, to a life of the whole centered perspective. And too, central to both, is work… real work… meaningful, dignifying work. We,

like all members, processes and systems of life, have purpose, role and work... work to sustain ourselves, to sustain our living, and to sustain the ongoingness of life – the whole of life, including human life - on earth... work required for realizing potential and our working in reciprocally nourishing ways... working in advancing humanness ways... working in ways that reflect congruence with intent and that which works for all children.

All of which brings us back to the necessity for seeing and understanding, and for the developing of our ableness with regard to that. Wholistic seeing and understanding is process; knowledge is structure. The rational mind, the reasoning mind of existence, can expand to add knowledge, manipulative knowledge; but it is not the mind of seeing and understanding intent and intended ways. Seeing and understanding is process, and comes from and through process - process not unlike that of intentional dialoguing. Seeing and understanding is accessible through process when we are actively present within and to the process.

Process is the domain of intuition, and at this time it is the intuition of wholeness that is being called upon; the intuition of wholeness being the developable means for accessing the wisdom of intent. Wisdom, being present to creation, understands intent and intended ways. This accessing and processing of and by the intuition of wholeness not only serves to make visible the path of original intent; but also, through the intentional, purposeful employment of reason, this path of original intent, this becoming path of advancing our

humanness, becomes possible and practice-able… unfolding before us in truly human ways – intentional ways of living and working.

And now we bring this writing to a close with images of our unfolding story… a story of our becoming an intentional people… a truly fruitful people of earth, people who are living and working in life nourishing ways… a people breathing vitality and viability into the struggling and dying earth. Thus our story becomes more and more a story of truth… a story of a people who themselves were saved from death… saved from lasting death through a process of being returned to life, reconnected to life – to the Source of life and to the whole of life… a people who seek to fully and ongoingly embrace the truth of our livingness, our intended membership in the community of life… a people who, through the exercise of conscious choice – that uniquely human capacity – turned away from gaining manipulative knowledge, turned away from seeking to bend the future towards desires of existence… and willfully turned hearts and minds towards ways of harmony and congruence with intended ways of working of life on this earth; and towards pursuits that work for all children in the world… ways and pursuits made visible and actionable through a life of the whole perspective of the works and the word.

www.pathofpotential.org
www.facebook.com/pathofpotential

THE GOING FORWARD YES

43

Redemption... Being Reborn in, of and through Spirit – the Spirit

Redemption. Our being redeemed is a process... a called for process of now... an unfolding process that requires an authentic yes on our part - an authentic yes to original intent... requires our saying "Yes" to the whole of the truth of the Source: the truth of all-inclusive love; the truth of our being, through intent of the Source, created as creatures of life; the truth of our emerging from one Source - the Source of love, the Source of life... the living Source of each and all...

Redemption... being a process of our saying "Yes" to our work and role - work and role with regard to the ongoingness of life... calling for a committed yes; a yes of the community to joining in the work of the Father - the eternalizing of life on and through the earth work of the Father, the Creator, the intentional Source of all... a process requiring our being and becoming vessels for the all-inclusive love of the Source entering into the working of the world of our making such that what we create is a manifestation of intent - the intent of the Source...

Redemption... a process that follows the pattern of all true shifts in being - real steps along the path of our becoming an authentic people of the Source, an intentional people of earth... a process, an unfolding process, of elevating dialoguing... a process that requires seeing and seeking wholeness, and requires the accessing of the wisdom of intent... a process, not of structure and hierarchy, but rather one of, through and

within community... a process that requires we see Christ as process; and seek to see and understand intended ways of working of life on this living earth...

Redemption... a process that requires an authentic yes... a process that authentically answers – through heart and mind – the critical question of our time:

Was our being saved all about us – only that; or was there some higher intentional purpose?

www.pathofpotential.org
www.facebook.com/pathofpotential

45

Our Return... Our Willful Returning to the Path of Original Intent

+ Whereas it is through grace - the un-earnable grace of the Source - that we are saved...

+ And it is through love - the all-inclusive unconditioned love of the Source - entering into and through our processes*, that our potential and the potential of the whole of life is unfolded... is realized...

> *processes that require we move beyond - enfold within, but move beyond - the limitations of instinctive love, the instinctive love of self, family, tribe, etc.... processes that require our moving towards oneness and wholeness.

+ It is through work, called work – our taking up of intentional ways of working and living – that we worship in spirit and truth... thus moving ourselves towards the fulfilling of the prophecy of Christ:

> *"The hour is coming, and is now here,*
> *when true worshippers*
> *will worship the Father in spirit and truth;*
> *And indeed,*
> *the Father seeks such people to worship him."*
> (John 4:23)

All of this – our willful returning to the path of original intent; the fulfilling of our intentional purpose – requires that we move beyond the limitations of reason, reasoned interpretation; that we come from a life of the whole perspective; and calls for our seeking to access the wisdom of intent... a process which itself

requires the accessing and developing of the intuition of wholeness.

And ultimately... our returning – our moving towards the whole of the truth of the Source – calls upon, requires us, to have faith... faith in intent... faith in original intent... a faith such that we seek congruence with, mastery of, intended ways; rather than mastery over pursuits... a congruence that is reflected in our working to create a culture that works for all children in the world... a faith in intent, in original intent, that awakens within, the realness and gravity of Christ's question regarding faith:

> *When I return, will I find one person of faith on the earth?*

(Ref. Luke 18:8)

47

A recapitulation...

Reflecting upon what is written here has evoked some imaging of the step change versus incremental improvement nature of what is now trying to unfold... the going forward nature of change behind the stirring more and more of us are innerly experiencing. A seeing and imagery that makes real the ground, the necessary ground for the work before us... the necessary ground of our having faith in intent, faith in love, faith in life... faith in the whole of the truth of the Source. The seeing of a truthfully new path, a path we are being called towards, is becoming present, actively present. An increasing clarity of path – the path of original intent... a path not of fear – not to be taken in fear – but rather a path of love, of love in the process, the all-inclusive love of the Source... the love through which all things are possible.

Terry

www.pathofpotential.org
www.facebook.com/pathofpotential

48

*From the time we pridefully
left the Garden,*

*the aim of the Source for
all interactions with humanity*

has been and continues to be

*our willful returning to
the path of Original Intent...*

*...a process which ultimately
requires the exercising of our
uniquely human, our truly human,
capacities of conscious choice
and free will.*

www.pathofpotential.org
www.facebook.com/pathofpotential

Books from
Path of Potential

The Becoming Intentional People Series:

BECOMING AN INTENTIONAL PEOPLE OF EARTH

ADVANCING OUR HUMANNESS... Choosing a Path of Congruence with Intent

INTENTIONAL GRANDMOTHERING... Choosing the Life Philosophy that Works for all Children in the World

The Desert Series:

WORK FOR ALL CHILDREN

DEVELOPING PLANETARY ETHICS; The Urgent Work of Today's Generation

WHO WILL SPEAK FOR EARTH? Reflections on Securing Energy from a Life of the Whole Perspective

AT THIS TIME OF POTENTIAL

Other Writings from Path of Potential:

The Library of Living Potential:
www.pathofpotential.org

Path of Potential on Facebook:
www.facebook.com/pathofpotential

To order books, go to the Path of Potential website, or call:
Melody Fraser, The Mail Suite, 1-800-818-6177 or 1-970-241-8973

Path of Potential
TS Potential, LLC
P.O. Box 4058
Grand Junction, CO 81502 USA
www.pathofpotential.org
email: editor@pathofpotential.org